DATA MINING IN TIME SERIES AND STREAMING DATABASES

SERIES IN MACHINE PERCEPTION AND ARTIFICIAL INTELLIGENCE*

ISSN: 1793-0839

Editors: **H. Bunke** (University of Bern, Switzerland)
P. S. P. Wang (Northeastern University, USA)
Joseph Lladós (Autonomous University of Barcelona, Spain)

This book series addresses all aspects of machine perception and artificial intelligence. Of particular interest are the areas of pattern recognition, image processing, computer vision, natural language understanding, speech processing, neural computing, machine learning, hardware architectures, software tools, and others. The series includes publications of various types, for example, textbooks, monographs, edited volumes, conference and workshop proceedings, PhD theses with significant impact, and special issues of the International Journal of Pattern Recognition and Artificial Intelligence.

Published

*The complete list of the published volumes in the series can be found at
http://www.worldscientific.com/series/smpai

Series in Machine Perception and Artificial Intelligence – Vol. 83

DATA MINING IN TIME SERIES AND STREAMING DATABASES

Editors

Mark Last
Ben-Gurion University of the Negev, Israel

Horst Bunke
University of Bern, Switzerland

Abraham Kandel
University of South Florida, USA

World Scientific

NEW JERSEY · LONDON · SINGAPORE · BEIJING · SHANGHAI · HONG KONG · TAIPEI · CHENNAI

Published by

World Scientific Publishing Co. Pte. Ltd.

5 Toh Tuck Link, Singapore 596224

USA office: 27 Warren Street, Suite 401-402, Hackensack, NJ 07601

UK office: 57 Shelton Street, Covent Garden, London WC2H 9HE

Library of Congress Cataloging-in-Publication Data

Names: Last, Mark, editor. | Bunke, Horst, 1949–   editor. | Kandel, Abraham, editor.

Title: Data mining in time series and streaming databases / edited by Mark Last
   (Ben-Gurion University of the Negev, Israel), Horst Bunke (University of Bern, Switzerland),
   Abraham Kandel (University of South Florida, USA).

Description: [Hackensack] New Jersey : World Scientific, [2018] | Series: Series in machine
   perception and artificial intelligence ; volume 83 | Includes bibliographical references.

Identifiers: LCCN 2017044537 | ISBN 9789813228030 (hc : alk. paper)

Subjects: LCSH: Data mining. | Big data. | Streaming technology (Telecommunications) |
   Electronic data processing--Distributed processing. | Querying (Computer science)

Classification: LCC QA76.9.D343 D38328 2018 | DDC 006.3/12--dc23

LC record available at https://lccn.loc.gov/2017044537

British Library Cataloguing-in-Publication Data

A catalogue record for this book is available from the British Library.

For any available supplementary material, please visit
http://www.worldscientific.com/worldscibooks/10.1142/10655#t=suppl

Desk Editor: Herbert Moses

Typeset by Stallion Press
Email: enquiries@stallionpress.com

Printed in Singapore

To my wife Tami, my parents Rosa and Isidore, and our children Dan,
Iris, and Einat.

M.L.

To my wife Helga.

H.B.

To my wife Nurit, our children Sharon, Gill and Adi, their spouses Gili,
Donna and Karen, and our grandchildren Kfeer,
Maya, Riley, Liam, Leo, Marley.

A.K.

Preface

Most data mining and machine learning algorithms are designed to deal with "static" data, which is stored entirely in a database system and which does not change significantly over time. Many such algorithms even ignore the arrival ordering of observations as irrelevant to the knowledge discovery process. With these assumptions being sufficiently accurate in some applications, an increasing amount of systems and sensors produce massive, high-speed streams of ever-changing data generated by dynamic processes. The high volume and velocity of such data streams require real time or near real time processing due to the volatility of the incoming observations, which can be stored for a limited, if any, time only. Dynamic data streams can be found in a variety of fields including weather monitoring, traffic control, stock trading, cyber security, and more recently, Internet of Things (IoT). Mining real-world time series and streaming data creates a need for new technologies and algorithms, which are currently being developed and tested by data scientists worldwide.

This volume is a continuation of our previous editorial project — *Data Mining in Time Series Databases* (*World Scientific*, 2004), which discussed the aspects and challenges introduced to the tasks of data mining and knowledge discovery by adding the time dimension to databases. The purpose of the current volume is to present the significant progress made over the last decade in pre-processing, mining, and utilization of streaming data. Data stream mining researchers are working on multiple tasks such as finding the most efficient representation of streaming data, developing privacy-preserving methods for data stream mining, incremental pre-processing of continuous time series and data streams in parallel to the data mining process, handling delayed information, mining entity-related time series, and developing online monitoring systems. Our book covers the state-of-the-art research in some of these areas. Specific topics discussed by the authors of this volume are described below.

Chapter 1 by Albert Bifet, Jesse Read, Geoff Holmes, and Bernhard Pfahringer describes Massive Online Analytics (MOA), an open source software environment for implementing algorithms and running experiments for online learning from evolving data streams. MOA is designed to deal with the challenging problem of scaling up the implementation of state-of-the-art algorithms to Big Data. The chapter discusses several change detection techniques implemented in MOA along with classification and clustering algorithms for streaming data. The current plans for extending MOA by its core team and the community developers conclude this chapter.

Chapter 2 by Douglas Cardoso, Felipe França, and Joao Gama deals with the problem of data stream mining under limited computational resources. To reduce the computation costs, they propose to use Weightless Artificial Neural Networks (WANNs), which contrary to standard ANNs, have no weights on their links. The authors present a learning algorithm based on the WiSARD (Wilkes, Stonham and Aleksander Recognition Device) methodology and apply it to the data stream clustering task. Finally, they indicate that many more potential applications of the WiSARD model to data streams still need to be explored.

In Chapter 3, Dariusz Brzezinski and Jerzy Stefanowski discuss another challenging problem — classification of non-stationary data streams where one of the target classes is represented by much less instances than other classes. Due to the evolving nature of non-stationary data streams, their class imbalance situation may change over time along with a change in decision boundaries known as a *concept drift*. The chapter describes recent advances in the field of imbalanced data streams classification. Besides presenting the current state-of-the-art in ensemble algorithms for imbalanced streams, the authors stress the limitations of existing approaches and outline new research directions.

Chapter 4 by Andreas Nienkötter and Xiaoyi Jiang deals with consensus learning for sequence data, especially strings. In multiple classifier combination, consensus methods produce a result, which best represents the different classifier predictions and thus removes errors and outliers in the input ensemble. As indicated by the chapter authors, strings provide a simple and yet powerful representation scheme for time series and other types of sequential data. A typical data-mining task is to represent a set of similar objects by means of a single prototype (median). The chapter briefly describes several procedures for computing median strings. Experimental results are reported to demonstrate the median concept and to compare some of the discussed algorithms.

In Chapter 5, Mark Last, Maxim Stoliar, and Menahem Friedman present a clustering-based methodology for efficient classification of stationary document streams. They propose an active learning algorithm, which obtains a continuous stream of unlabeled documents and clusters them incrementally so that each incoming document is inserted into an existing cluster or used to start a new cluster of its own. Occasionally, an expert is called to label some clusters for the classification mechanism. The evaluation experiments on two benchmark corpora show that active learning combined with clustering can reduce the labeling costs by increasing the percentage of automatically categorized documents over time.

Chapter 6 by Remon Cornelisse and Sunil Choenni illustrates the importance of domain knowledge in the interpretation and extraction of knowledge from data streams. The authors use examples of time series from the completely diverse fields of cyber security, astronomy, and criminal justice. The chapter focus is on the first two stages of the knowledge discovery process — data selection and data pre-processing.

Finally, Chapter 7 by Mohsin Munir, Sebastian Baumbach, Ying Gu, Andreas Dengel, and Sheraz Ahmed provides a comprehensive overview of data stream and time series analytics used by various industries for improving healthcare services, enhancing home security, increasing crop yield, expediting goods delivery, reducing equipment downtime, avoiding diseases, and other purposes. Most of these solutions are utilizing the streaming/time-series data coming from IoT enabled devices. The authors suggest that the existing solutions can be further enhanced by means of advanced machine learning techniques like the deep learning.

As becomes evident from the chapters of this book, time series and streaming data keeps presenting new challenges to data scientists in academia and industry. Most data streams are characterized by all the four famous V's of Big Data (Volume, Variety, Velocity, and Veracity), often combined with the fifth V — the Volatility of the dynamic environment. The contributors of this volume have provided their insights on some state-of-the-art solutions for mining Big Streaming Data as well as on the topics for future research in this exciting area.

Mark Last
Horst Bunke
Abraham Kandel
July 2017

About the Editors

 **Abraham Kandel** received a B.Sc. from the Technion-Israel Institute of Technology and an M.S. from the University of California, both in Electrical Engineering, and he also holds a Ph.D. in Electrical Engineering and Computer Science from the University of New Mexico. Dr. Kandel is a Distinguished Emeritus Professor in Computer Science and Engineering at the University of South Florida, Tampa, FL, USA. He has been the Department Chairman (1991–2003), the Executive Director of the National Institute for Applied Computational Intelligence, Founding Chairman of the Computer Science Department at Florida State University (1978–1991), Director of the Institute of Expert Systems and Robotics, and Director of the State University System Center for Artificial Intelligence at FSU. He is the Editor of the Fuzzy Track — *IEEE MICRO*; Area Editor on Fuzzy Hardware for *Fuzzy Sets and Systems*, Associate Editor of *IEEE Transactions on Systems, Man, and Cybernetics, Control Engineering Practice*, and *International Journal of Pattern Recognition and Artificial Intelligence* (IJPRAI). Dr. Kandel has published over 900 refereed papers and is an author, co-author, editor, or co-editor of 51 textbooks and research monographs in the field. Dr. Kandel is a Fellow of ACM, IEEE, New York Academy of Sciences, AAAS, and IFSA, and a member of NAFIPS, IAPR, ASEE, and Sigma-Xi. He is a recipient of IEEE Pioneer Award in 2012 and Fay and Lotfi Zadeh Lifetime Achievement Award in 2016 (SDPS).

Horst Bunke joined the University of Bern as a Professor of Computer Science in 1984. He is a Professor Emeritus, and his areas of interest include pattern recognition and artificial intelligence. He served as the first Vice-President and Acting President of the International Association for Pattern Recognition (IAPR). He also is a former Editor-in-Charge of the *International Journal of Pattern Recognition and Artificial Intelligence* and a former member of the editorial board of various journals. Horst is the recipient of the 2010 KS Fu Prize, awarded by the IAPR. Moreover, he received the IAPR/ICDAR Outstanding Achievements Award in 2009 and an honorary doctoral degree from the University of Szeged, Hungary, in 2007. He has more than 700 publications, including over 40 authored, co-authored, edited, or co-edited books and special editions of journals.

Mark Last is a Full Professor at the Department of Software and Information Systems Engineering, Ben-Gurion University of the Negev, Israel and the Head of the Data Science and Text Mining Group. Prof. Last obtained his Ph.D. degree from Tel Aviv University, Israel in 2000. During the years 2009–2012, Prof. Last has served as the Head of the Software Engineering Program at Ben-Gurion University. He has published over 190 peer-reviewed papers and 10 books on data mining, text mining, and cyber security. Prof. Last is a Senior Member of the IEEE Computer Society and a Professional Member of the Association for Computing Machinery (ACM). He currently serves as an Associate Editor of *IEEE Transactions on Cybernetics* and an Editorial Board Member of *Data Mining and Knowledge Discovery*. From 2007 to 2016, he has served as an Associate Editor of *Pattern Analysis and Applications*. His main research interests are focused on data mining, cross-lingual text mining, cyber intelligence, and medical informatics.

About the Contributors

Albert Bifet is an Associate Professor at Telecom Paris Tech and an Honorary Research Associate at the WEKA Machine Learning Group at University of Waikato. Previously, he worked at Huawei Noah's Ark Lab in Hong Kong, Yahoo Labs in Barcelona, University of Waikato, and UPC Barcelona Tech. He is the author of the book, *Adaptive Stream Mining: Pattern Learning and Mining from Evolving Data Streams*. He is one of the leaders of MOA and Apache SAMOA software environments for implementing algorithms and running experiments for online learning from evolving data streams. He served as a Co-Chair of the Industrial track of IEEE MDM 2016, ECML PKDD 2015, and as Co-Chair of BigMine (2017–2012), and ACM SAC Data Streams Track (2018–2012).

Professor Andreas Dengel is a member of the Management Board as well as Scientific Director at the German Research Center for Artificial Intelligence (DFKI) in Kaiserslautern where he leads the Smart Data & Knowledge Services Research Department. In 1993, he became a Professor at the Computer Science Department, University of Kaiserslautern. Since 2009, he also holds an Honorary Professorship at the Department of Computer Science and Intelligent Systems, Graduate School of Engineering, Osaka Prefecture University. Prof. Dengel has headed numerous international research and development projects and conferences and is the founder and initiator of several successful start-up companies. He has received several international awards for his research.

Andreas Nienkötter received his Master's degree in Computer Science from the University of Münster, Germany in 2015. Since then, he has been a Ph.D. student in Prof. Xiaoyi Jiang's research group for Pattern Recognition and Image Analysis (PRIA) at the University of Münster. His research interests include consensus learning using the generalized median, vector space embedding, and dimensionality reduction methods.

Bernhard Pfahringer received his Ph.D. degree from the University of Technology in Vienna, Austria in 1995. He is currently a Professor with the Department of Computer Science at the University of Waikato, New Zealand. His interests span a range of data mining and machine learning sub-fields, with a focus on streaming, randomization, and complex data. He has published extensively in the data stream mining field since 2005.

Dariusz Brzezinski received his M.Sc. and Ph.D. degrees in Computer Science from Poznan University of Technology, Poland, in 2010 and 2015, respectively. During this time, his main research was focused on structure-based clustering of XML data and the development of classifier ensembles for time-changing data streams. Currently, he is an Assistant Professor in the Department of Data Processing Technologies at Poznan University of Technology, where his research is focused on data stream mining, concept drift detection, class imbalance, classifier evaluation measures, and machine learning applications in X-ray crystallography.

Douglas O. Cardoso is an Assistant Professor at the Department of Computer Engineering of CEFET-RJ Petrópolis, Brazil. He received his B.Sc. in Computer Science and M.Sc. and Ph.D. in Computer and Systems Engineering in 2009, 2012, and 2017, respectively, all from Federal University of Rio de Janeiro (UFRJ). His research interests include clustering, open set recognition, data streams mining, and weightless neural networks.

Felipe M. G. França is Professor of Computer Science and Engineering, COPPE, Federal University of Rio de Janeiro (UFRJ), Brazil. He received his degree in Electronics Engineering from UFRJ (1982), an M.Sc. in Computer Science from COPPE/UFRJ (1987), and his Ph.D. from the Department of Electrical and Electronics Engineering, Imperial College London, U.K. (1994). He has research and teaching interests in computational intelligence, distributed algorithms, sensor networks, dataflow computing, and other aspects of parallel and distributed computing.

Geoff Holmes is currently the Dean of the Faculty of Computing and Mathematical Sciences at the University of Waikato, New Zealand. He obtained B.Sc. and Ph.D. degrees in Mathematics from Southampton University, U.K. in 1986. After time spent as a research assistant at the University of Cambridge, he joined Waikato in 1987; after moving up the ranks, he was promoted to Professor in 2008. He has made contributions in machine learning across several branches of the subject and has been active in finding ways to reward researchers for their efforts to produce open source software. In this regard, he acts as an Action Editor for the branch of *JMLR* dedicated to open source software.

 **Jerzy Stefanowski** received his M.Sc degree in control engineering from Poznań University of Technology in 1987. The same year, he joined Intelligent Decision Support System Lab in the Institute of Computing Science at the same university. He defended his Ph.D. and Habilitation theses in computer science (in 1994 and 2001, respectively) also at Poznań University of Technology, where he currently works as an Associate Professor of Computer Science. His research interests include machine learning, data mining, and intelligent decision support — in particular, rule induction, multiple classifiers, class imbalance, concept drift, classification of data streams, clustering algorithms, and methods for Big Data. Over the course of his work, he participated in several projects with Polish and European funding. Moreover, he was an invited professor or visiting researcher at several European universities. In addition to his research activities, he has served in a number of organizational capacities: former President of Wielkopolska Regional Branch of Polish Information Processing Society (2006–2011), current member and Vice-President of the Executive Board of Polish Artificial Intelligence Society; and also co-founder and co-leader of Polish Special Interest Group on Machine Learning. Moreover, he has been the Editor in Chief of the journal *Foundations of Computing and Decision Science* since 2012.

For more information, please refer to {`http://www.cs.put.poznan.pl/jstefanowski`}

Jesse Read is an Assistant Professor in the DaSciM group at l'Ecole Polytechnique in France. He obtained his Ph.D. in 2010 in the machine learning group at the University of Waikato in New Zealand. He then began post-doctoral research in the University Carlos III of Madrid. Since 2013, he has been at Aalto University in Helsinki. Aside from multi-label classification, his research interests include learning from sequential data, evolving data streams, and working with applications of sensory data. He is the leader of the MEKA open source software project.

João Gama received his Ph.D. in Computer Science in 2000. He is a senior researcher at INESC TEC. He has worked in several National and European projects on Incremental and Adaptive Learning Systems, Ubiquitous Knowledge Discovery, Learning from Massive and Structured Data, etc. He served as the Program Chair at several machine learning and data mining conferences. He is the author of a monograph *Knowledge Discovery from Data Streams* and has published more than 200 peer-reviewed papers in areas related to machine learning, data mining, and data streams.

Max Stoliar received his Bachelor's degree in Computer Science from the Ben-Gurion University in 2004. From 2004 to 2011, he worked as Tech Leader and Architect in the IDF. During this period, he received his MBA specializing in Entrepreneurship and Hi-Tech, and commenced his M.Sc. in Information Systems Engineering, which he completed in 2013 with a thesis in the subject of *Clustering-Based Classification of Documents with Active Learning*

under the supervision of Prof. Mark Last and Dr. Menachem Friedman. Recently, he has worked at leading international firms as Tech Lead and VP R&D in the fields of social and professional networks, security, and finance.

Born in 1940, **Menahem Friedman** received his M.Sc. in Mathematics from the Hebrew University in 1962. In 1967, he obtained his Ph.D. in Applied Mathematics from the Weizmann Institute. After two years spent as a Post-Doc at the Department of Computer Science, University of Minnesota, USA, Friedman started working at the Nuclear Research Center and at the Ben Gurion University in Israel until his retirement in 2006. Friedman has written ten three books and published over 100 papers on numerical analysis and artificial intelligence.

Mohsin Munir received his Master's degree in Computer Science from the University of Kaiserslautern, Germany. He has interned at RICOH (Japan) and BOSCH (Germany) during his Master's degree. The topic of his Master's thesis was "Connected Heating Systems' Fault Detection using Data Anomalies and Trends". Currently, he is pursuing his Ph.D. in Computer Science at German Research Center for Artificial Intelligence (DFKI GmbH) under the supervision of Prof. Dr. Prof. H. C. Andreas Dengel. His research topic is "Time Series Forecasting and Anomaly Detection". His research interests are time series analysis, deep neural networks, forecasting, predictive analytics, and anomaly detection. During his Ph.D., he did a research internship at Kyushu University (Japan) under the supervision of Prof. Seiichi Uchida.

Rémon Cornelisse received his Ph.D. in Astrophysics from the University of Utrecht (the Netherlands) in 2003. His main interest during his Ph.D. was time series analysis of continuous observations from an X-ray satellite. He continued his work on time series analysis of astrophysical objects at the University of Southampton (Great Britain) and the Canarian Astronomical Institute (Spain) using European and Spanish funding before moving back to the Netherlands to work for the Department of Security and Justice. Using a Dutch grant, he exploited his expertise to work on time series analysis of internet traffic for cyber security purposes. In particular, he explored the possibilities to extract relevant information at the strategic level from the large amounts of security data that are produced.

Sebastian Baumbach received his Master's degree in Computer Science from the University of Magdeburg (Germany). The topic of this Masters' thesis was "Spatio-temporal Clustering of Trajectories to Detect Activity and Behavior Patterns of People". Currently, he is pursuing a Ph.D. in the German Research Center for Artificial Intelligence (DFKI GmbH), under the supervision of Prof. Dr. Prof. H.C. Andreas Dengel. His Ph.D. is on Conceptualization of Contextual Geospatial-temporal Data for Decision Support Systems. His research interest includes data mining, spatial data, activity recognition, sensor data, time series analysis, and deep learning. His private start-up company produces an early disease recognition system for cows by utilizing modern AI, cloud, and sensor technologies. There, he is leading the development of the main research line on how to analyze multi-dimensional multi-model data from cows and dairy farms in order to give recommendations to farmers.

Dr. Sheraz Ahmed received his Master's degree from the University of Kaiserslautern, Germany and Ph.D. in the German Research Center for Artificial Intelligence (DFKI GmbH), Germany, under the supervision of Prof. Dr. H.C. Andreas Dengel and Prof. Dr. habil. Marcus Liwicki. His Ph.D. topic was Generic Methods for Information Segmentation in Document Images. His research interests include document understanding, generic segmentation framework for documents, time series analysis, gesture recognition, pattern recognition, data mining, anomaly detection, and natural language processing. He has more than 20 publications on the aforesaid topics and other related ones, including three journal papers and two book chapters. He is a frequent reviewer of various journals and conferences including *Pattern Recognition Letters, Neural Computing and Applications, IJDAR, ICDAR, ICFHR, DAS*, and so on.

Sunil Choenni holds a Ph.D. in database technology from the University of Twente and an M.Sc. in theoretical computer science from the Delft University of Technology. Currently, he is heading the Department of Statistical Information Management and Policy Analysis of the Research and Documentation Centre (WODC) of the Dutch Ministry of Security and Justice. Furthermore, he is a Professor in the field of Smart and Inclusive Society at Rotterdam University of Applied Sciences, Rotterdam. Prior to joining WODC, he held several teaching and research positions at different universities and research centers. His research interests include data warehouses and data mining, databases, e-government, cyber security, and human-centered design.

Xiaoyi Jiang studied computer science at Peking University and received his Ph.D. and *Venia Docendi* (Habilitation) degree in Computer Science from the University of Bern, Switzerland. He was an Associate Professor at Technical University of Berlin, Germany. Since 2002, he is a Full Professor of Computer Science at University of Münster, Germany, and currently Dean of the Faculty of Mathematics and Computer Science. He is Editor-in-Chief of *International Journal of Pattern Recognition and Artificial Intelligence*. In addition, he also serves on the Advisory Board and Editorial Board of several journals, including *IEEE Transactions on Medical Imaging, International Journal of Neural Systems, Pattern Analysis and Applications*, and *Pattern Recognition*. His research interests include biomedical imaging, 3D image analysis, and structural pattern recognition. He is a Senior Member of IEEE and a Fellow of IAPR.

Ying Gu comes from Shanghai, China. After finishing her Bachelor's degree in Management from Chongqing Technology and Business University in China, she began to study mathematics in Germany and received her Master's Degree in Mathematics from the Heidelberg University. She is a Ph.D. student at the University of Kaiserslautern under the supervision of Prof. Dr. Prof. H.C. Andreas Dengel and works as an Assistant Researcher in the German Research Center for Artificial Intelligence (DFKI GmbH). Her research interests are mainly focused on anomaly detection for large datasets and sensor data.

Contents

Chapter 1

Streaming Data Mining with Massive Online Analytics (MOA)

Albert Bifet

LTCI, Télécom ParisTech
Université Paris-Saclay, France
albert.bifet@telecom-paristech.fr

Jesse Read

LIX, École Polytechnique
Université Paris-Saclay, France
jesse.read@polytechnique.edu

Geoff Holmes* and Bernhard Pfahringer[†]

Computer Science Department
University of Waikato, New Zealand
*geoff@waikato.ac.nz
[†]bernhard@waikato.ac.nz

Fast Big Data is being produced at high-velocity in real-time. To effectively deal with this type of streaming data produced in real time, we need to be able to adapt to changes on the distribution of the data being produced, and we need to do it using the minimum amount of time and memory. The Internet of Things (IoT) is a good example and motivation of this type of streaming data produced in real time.

Massive Online Analytics (MOA) is a software environment for implementing algorithms and running experiments for online learning from evolving data streams. MOA is designed to deal with the challenging problem of scaling up the implementation of state of the art algorithms to real world dataset sizes. MOA includes classification and clustering methods. It contains collection of offline and online methods as well as tools for evaluation. MOA supports bi-directional interaction with WEKA, the Waikato Environment for Knowledge Analysis, and is released under the GNU GPL license.

1. Introduction

Nowadays, data is generated at an increasing rate from sensor applications, measurements in network monitoring and traffic management, log records or click-streams in web exploring, manufacturing processes, call detail records, email, blogging, twitter posts and others. In fact, all data generated can be considered as streaming data or as a snapshot of streaming data, since it is obtained from an interval of time.

In the data stream model, data arrive at high speed, and an algorithm must process them under very strict constraints of space and time. MOA is an open-source framework for dealing with massive, potentially infinite, evolving data streams.

A data stream environment has different requirements from the traditional batch learning setting. The most significant are the following:

Requirement 1 Process an example at a time, and inspect it only once (at most)

Requirement 2 Use a limited amount of memory

Requirement 3 Work in a limited amount of time

Requirement 4 Be ready to predict at any time.

Figure 1 illustrates the typical use of a data stream classification algorithm, and how the requirements fit in a repeating cycle:

(1) The algorithm is passed the next available example from the stream (Requirement 1).

(2) The algorithm processes the example, updating its data structures. It does so without exceeding the memory bounds set on it (requirement 2), and as quickly as possible (Requirement 3).

(3) The algorithm is ready to accept the next example. On request it is able to predict the class of unseen examples (Requirement 4).

As data stream mining is a relatively new field, evaluation practices are not nearly as well researched and established as they are in the traditional batch setting. The majority of experimental evaluations use less than one million training examples. In the context of data streams this is disappointing, because to be truly useful at data stream classification the algorithms need to be capable of handling very large (potentially infinite) streams of examples. Demonstrating systems only on small amounts of data does not build a convincing case for capacity to solve more demanding data stream applications [1].

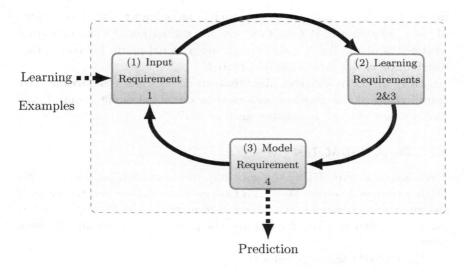

Fig. 1. The data stream classification cycle.

MOA permits evaluation of data stream learning algorithms on large streams, in the order of tens of millions of examples where possible, and under explicit memory limits. Any less than this does not actually test algorithms in a realistically challenging setting.

Other Machine Learning frameworks as Weka, RapidMiner or scikit-learn were not designed for data stream mining. In those frameworks, data is considered static, and can be stored in main memory. MOA was designed specifically for the data stream setting, with the challenging capabilities of adapting to changes and processing data without storing it.

2. Concept Drift

Dealing with data streams evolving over time, our models need to adapt to changes on the data. To do that, we need to know when it is the best moment to adapt them. This is why it is important to detect changes, in a fast and accurate way, so that we can update or replace our current models when it is more appropriate.

A *change detector* or *drift detector* is an algorithm that having as input a stream of instances, outputs an alarm if it detects change on the distribution of the data, and optionally a prediction of the next instance to come. In general, the input to this algorithm is a sequence $x_1, x_2, \ldots, x_t, \ldots$ of data items whose distribution varies over time in an unknown way. The outputs of the algorithm are, at each time step, an estimation of some important parameters of the input distribution, and a signal alarm indicating that distribution change has recently occurred.

There are many different algorithms to detect change in streams. We start looking at the classical ones used in statistical quality control, and then we look at more recent ones such as ADWIN.

2.1. *The CUSUM Test*

The cumulative sum (CUSUM algorithm), which was first proposed in 1954 [2], is a change detection algorithm that gives an alarm when the mean of the input data is significantly different from zero. The CUSUM input ϵ_t can be any filter residual, for instance the prediction error from a Kalman filter.

The CUSUM test is as follows:

$$g_0 = 0$$

$$g_t = \max\ (0, g_{t-1} + \epsilon_t - v)$$

$$\text{if } g_t > h \text{ then alarm and } g_t = 0$$

The CUSUM test is memoryless, and its accuracy depends on the choice of parameters v and h.

2.2. *The Page Hinckley Test*

The CUSUM test is a stopping rule. Other stopping rules exist. For example, the Page Hinckley test, also presented in [2]. The Page Hinckley Test is as follows, when the signal is increasing:

$$g_0 = 0, \qquad g_t = g_{t-1} + (\epsilon_t - v)$$

$$G_t = \min(g_t)$$

$$\text{if } g_t - G_t > h \text{ then alarm and } g_t = 0$$

In the case that the signal is decreasing, instead of $G_t = \min(g_t)$, we should use $G_t = \max(g_t)$ and $G_t - g_t > h$ as the stopping rule. As the CUSUM test, the Page Hinckley test is memoryless, and its accuracy depends on the choice of parameters v and h.

2.3. *Drift Detection Method*

The drift detection method (DDM) proposed by Gama *et al.* [3] controls the number of errors produced by the learning model during prediction. It compares the statistics of two windows: the first contains all the data, and the second contains only the data from the beginning until the number of errors increases. Their method doesn't store these windows in memory. It keeps only statistics and a window of recent errors.

The number of errors in a sample of n examples is modelled by a binomial distribution. For each point t in the sequence that is being sampled, the error rate is the probability of misclassifying (p_t), with standard deviation given by $s_t = \sqrt{p_t(1 - p_t)/t}$. They assume that the error rate of the learning algorithm (p_t) will decrease while the number of examples increases if the distribution of the examples is stationary. A significant increase in the error of the algorithm, suggests that the class distribution is changing and, hence, the actual decision model is considered to be inappropriate. Thus, they store the values of p_t and s_t when $p_t + s_t$ reaches its minimum value during the process (obtaining p_{pmin} and s_{min}). And it checks when the following conditions trigger:

- $p_t + s_t \geq p_{min} + 2 \cdot s_{min}$ for the warning level. Beyond this level, the examples are stored in anticipation of a possible change of context.
- $p_t + s_t \geq p_{min} + 3 \cdot s_{min}$ for the drift level. Beyond this level the concept drift is considered to be real, the model induced by the learning method is reset and a new model is learnt using the examples stored since the warning level triggered. The values for p_{min} and s_{min} are reset too.

This approach demonstrates good behavior detecting abrupt changes and gradual changes when the gradual change is not very slow, but it has difficulties when the change is slowly gradual. In that case, the examples will be stored for a long time, the drift level can take too much time to trigger and the examples in memory can be excessive.

2.4. *ADWIN*

ADWIN (ADaptive sliding WINdow) [4] is a change detector and estimation algorithm. It solves, in a well-specified way, the problem of tracking the average of a stream of bits or real-valued numbers. ADWIN keeps a variable-length window of recently seen items, with the property that the window has the maximal length statistically consistent with the hypothesis "there has been no change in the average value inside the window".

More precisely, an older fragment of the window is dropped if and only if there is enough evidence that its average value differs from that of the rest of the window. This has two consequences: one, change is reliably detected whenever the window shrinks; and two, at any time the average over the existing window can be used as a reliable estimate of the current average in the stream (barring a very small or recent change that is not yet statistically significant).

The inputs to ADWIN are a confidence value $\delta \in (0, 1)$ and a (possibly infinite) sequence of real values x_1, x_2, x_3, ..., x_t, ... The value of x_t is available only at time t. Each x_t is generated according to some distribution D_t, independently for every t. We denote with μ_t the expected value of x_t when it is drawn according to D_t. We assume that x_t is always in $[0, 1]$; rescaling deals with cases where $a \leq x_t \leq b$. No further assumption is being made about the distribution D_t; in particular, μ_t is unknown for all t.

ADWIN is parameter- and assumption-free in the sense that it automatically detects and adapts to the current rate of change. Its only parameter is a confidence bound δ, indicating how confident we want to be in the algorithm's output, inherent to all algorithms dealing with random processes.

It is important to note that ADWIN does not maintain the window explicitly, but compresses it using a variant of the exponential histogram technique [5]. This means that it keeps a window of length W using only $O(\log W)$ memory and $O(\log W)$ processing time per item, rather than the $O(W)$ one expects from a naïve implementation.

3. Classification

Classification is one of the most widely used data mining techniques. In very general terms, given a list of groups (often called classes), classification seeks to predict to which group a new instance may belong. The outcome of classification is typically either the identification of a single group or the production of a probability distribution of likelihood of membership of each group. A spam filter is a good example, where we want to predict if new emails are considered spam or not. Twitter sentiment analysis is another example, where we want to predict if the sentiment of a new incoming tweet is positive or negative.

More formally, the classification problem can be formulated as follows: given a set of instances of the form (x, y), where $x = x_1, \ldots, x_k$ is a vector of attribute values, and y is a discrete class from a set of n_C different classes, the classifier builds a model $y = f(x)$ to predict the classes y of future examples. For example, x could be a tweet and y the polarity of its sentiment; or x could be an email message, and y the decision whether it is spam or not.

Evaluation is one of the most fundamental tasks in the stream data mining process, since it helps to decide what techniques are more appropriate to use for a specific data stream mining problem. The main challenge is to know when a method is outperforming another method only by chance, or if there is a statistical significance to that claim. Some of the methodologies applied are the same as in the case of non-dynamic data, where all data can be stored in memory. However, mining evolving data streams has new challenges and uses new evaluation methodologies. One thing worth noting before we continue is that almost all of the discoveries made in data mining and particularly classification assume that data is IID (Independent, Identically, Distributed). Thus a stationary distribution is randomly producing data, in no particular order and the underlying distribution generating the data is not changing. In a dynamic-data environment no part of IID remains valid. It is often the case, for example, that for certain time-periods the labels or classes of instances are correlated, intrusion detection has a majority of periods containing instance class labels designated no-intrusion and then shorter much less frequent periods of intrusion. This is another aspect of data stream mining that would benefit from further research.

For evolving data streams, the main difference with traditional data mining evaluation, is in how to perform the error estimation. Resources are limited and cross-validation may be too expensive.

The evaluation procedure of a learning algorithm determines which examples are used for training the algorithm, and which are used for testing the model output by the algorithm.

In traditional batch learning the problem of limited data is overcome by analyzing and averaging multiple models produced with different random arrangements of training and test data. In the stream setting the problem of (effectively) unlimited data poses different challenges.

When considering what procedure to use in the non-distributed data stream setting, one of the unique concerns is how to build a picture of accuracy over time. Two main approaches arise:

- **Holdout**: when data is so abundant, that it is possible to have test sets periodically, then we can measure the performance on these holdout sets. There is a training data stream that is used to train the learner continuously, and small test data sets that are used to compute the performance periodically.

- **Interleaved Test-Then-Train or Prequential**: when data is not abundant, and there are no test sets, then each individual example can be used to test the model *before* it is used for training, and from this the accuracy can be incrementally updated. The model is always being tested on examples it has not seen.

Holdout evaluation gives a more accurate estimation of the accuracy of the classifier on more recent data. However, it requires recent test data that it is difficult to obtain for real datasets. There is also the issue of ensuring coverage of important change events, if the holdout is during a less volatile period of change then it might give an over-estimate of classifier performance. Gama *et al.* [6] propose to use a forgetting mechanism for estimating holdout accuracy using prequential accuracy: a sliding window of size w with the most recent observations, or fading factors that weigh observations using a decay factor α. The output of the two mechanisms is very similar (every window of size w_0 may be approximated by some decay factor α_0).

In a distributed data stream setting, we have classifiers that can be trained at the same time. The approaches in this setting are the following [7]:

- k-**fold distributed split-validation**: when there is abundance of data and k classifiers. Each time a new instance arrive, it is decided with probability $1/k$ if it will be used for testing. If it is used for testing, it is used by all the classifiers. If not, then it is used for training and assigned to only one classifier. Doing that, each classifier sees different instances, and they are tested using the same data.
- 5×2 **distributed cross-validation**: when data is less abundant, and we want to use only 10 classifiers. We have 5 groups of 2 classifiers, and for each group, each time a new instance arrive, it is decided with probability $1/2$ which of the two classifiers is used to test; the other classifier of the group is used to train. All instances are used to test or to train, and there is no overlapping between test instances and train instances.
- k-**fold distributed cross-validation**: when data is scarce and we have k classifiers. Each time a new instance arrive, it is used for testing in one classifier selected randomly, and trained using the others. This is the equivalent evaluation to k-fold distributed cross-validation.

The *decision tree* is a very popular data mining technique since it is very easy to interpret and visualize the model it builds. It consists of a tree structure, where each internal node corresponds to an attribute that splits into a branch for each attribute value, and leaves correspond to classification predictors, usually majority class classifiers. Figure 2 shows an example.

Contains "Money"	Domain type	Has attach.	Time received	spam
yes	com	yes	night	yes
yes	edu	no	night	yes
no	com	yes	night	yes
no	edu	no	day	no
no	com	no	day	no
yes	cat	no	day	yes

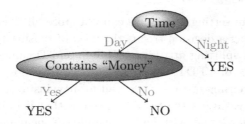

Fig. 2.   A data set that describes e-mail features for deciding if it is spam, and a decision tree build using this data set.

Decision tree accuracy performance can be improved, using other classifiers at the leaves, such as Naive Bayes, or using ensembles of classifiers, as we will see later on.

The basic way to build a tree is the following, starting by creating a root node at the beginning *node* = *root*, and then doing the following:

(1) Assign *A* as the best decision attribute for *node*.
(2) For each value of *A*, create new descendant of *node*.
(3) Sort training instances to leaf nodes.
(4) If training instances are perfectly classified, then STOP, else iterate over new leaf nodes.

Two common measures are used to select the best decision attribute:

- Information Gain: computed as the decrement in entropy

  Information Gain = Entropy(before Split) − Entropy(after split)

  where Entropy is a measure of the uncertainty associated with a random variable defined as Entropy = $-\sum^c p_i \cdot \log p_i$.
- Gini impurity Gain: computed using the Gini impurity measure instead of the entropy

$$\text{Gini Index} = \sum^c p_i(1 - p_i) = 1 - \sum^c p_i^2$$

The Gini index is a measure of the statistical dispersion associated with a random variable.

3.1. *The Hoeffding Tree*

In the data stream setting, where we can not store all the data, the main problem of building a decision tree is the need of reusing the examples to compute the best splitting attributes. Hulten and Domingos [8] proposed the Hoeffding Tree or VFDT, a very fast decision tree for streaming data, where instead of reusing instances, we wait for new instances to arrive. The most interesting feature of the Hoeffding tree is that it builds an identical tree with a traditional one, with high probability if the number of instances is large enough, and that it has theoretical guarantees about that.

The pseudo-code of VFDT is shown in Figure 3. The Hoeffding Tree is based on the Hoeffding bound. This inequality or bound justifies that a small sample can often be enough to choose an optimal splitting attribute. Suppose we make n independent observations of a random variable r with range R, where r is an attribute selection measure such as information gain or Gini impurity gain. The Hoeffding inequality states that with probability $1 - \delta$, if the true mean r of r is at least $E[r] - \epsilon$, then

$$\epsilon = \sqrt{\frac{R^2 \ln 1/\delta}{2n}}$$

Using this fact, the Hoeffding tree algorithm, can determine, with high probability the smallest number n of examples needed at a node when selecting a splitting attribute.

The Hoeffding Tree maintains in each node the statistics needed for splitting attributes. For discrete attributes, this is the same information as needed for computing the Naive Bayes predictions: a 3-dimensional table

HOEFFDINGTREE(*Stream*, δ)

1 ▷ Let HT be a tree with a single leaf(root)
2 ▷ Init counts n_{ijk} at root
3 **for** each example (x, y) in Stream
4   **do** HTGROW($(x, y), HT, \delta$)

HTGROW($(x, y), HT, \delta$)

1 ▷ Sort (x, y) to leaf l using HT
2 ▷ Update counts n_{ijk} at leaf l
3 **if** examples seen so far at l are not all of the same class
4   **then**
5   ▷ Compute G for each attribute
6   **if** $G(\text{Best Attr.}) - G(\text{2nd best}) > \sqrt{\frac{R^2 \ln 1/\delta}{2n}}$
7   **then**
8   ▷ Split leaf on best attribute
9   **for** each branch
10   **do** ▷ Start new leaf and initialize counts

Fig. 3. The Hoeffding Tree algorithm.

that stores for each triple (x_i, v_j, c) a count $n_{i,j,c}$ of training instances with $x_i = v_j$, together with a 1-dimensional table for the counts of $C = c$. The memory needed depends on the number of leaves of the tree, but not on the size of the data stream.

A theoretically appealing feature of Hoeffding Trees not shared by other incremental decision tree learners is that it has sound guarantees of performance. Using the Hoeffding bound one can show that its output is asymptotically nearly identical to that of a non-incremental learner using infinitely many examples.

Domingos *et al.* [8] improved the Hoeffding Tree algorithm with an extended method called VFDT, with the following characteristics:

- Ties: when two attributes have similar split gain G, the improved method splits if the Hoeffding bound computed is lower than a certain threshold parameter τ.

$$G(\text{Best Attr.}) - G(\text{2nd best}) < \sqrt{\frac{R^2 \ln 1/\delta}{2n}} < \tau$$

- To speed up the process, instead of computing the best attributes to split every time a new instance arrives, it computes them every time a number n_{min} of instances has arrived.
- To reduce the memory used in the mining, it deactivates the least promising nodes that have lower $p_l \times e_l$ where
  - p_l is the probability to reach leaf l
  - e_l is the error in the node l
  - It is possible to initialize the method with an appropriate decision tree. Hoeffding Trees can grow slowly and performance can be poor initially so this extension provides an immediate boost to the learning curve.

A way to improve the classification performance of the Hoeffding Tree is to use Naive Bayes learners at the leaves instead of the majority class classifier. Gama *et al.* [9] were the first to use Naive Bayes in Hoeffding Tree leaves, replacing the majority class classifier. However, Holmes *et al.* [10] identified situations where the Naive Bayes method outperformed the standard Hoeffding tree initially but is eventually overtaken. To solve that, they proposed a hybrid adaptive method that generally outperforms the two original prediction methods for both simple and complex concepts.

The Hoeffding Adaptive Tree [11] is an extension of the Hoeffding Tree that uses ADWIN as a change detector, to adapt the tree structure of the decision tree to the changes in the distribution of the learning data. Users can use the Hoeffding Adaptive Tree easily without needing to set parameters that depend on the scale of the data change.

3.2. *Ensemble Methods*

Ensemble methods are combinations of several models whose individual predictions are combined in some manner (e.g., averaging or voting) to form a final prediction. When tackling non-stationary concepts, ensembles of classifiers have several advantages over single classifier methods: they are easy to scale and parallelize, they can adapt to change quickly by pruning under-performing parts of the ensemble, and they therefore usually also generate more accurate concept descriptions.

Bagging, boosting and stacking are traditional ensemble methods for non-streaming environments. Usually ensemble methods outperform single classifiers at the cost of more time and memory resources.

Bagging is one of the simplest ensemble methods to implement. Non-streaming bagging [12] builds a set of M base models, training each model with a bootstrap sample of size N created by drawing random samples with replacement from the original training set. Each base model's training set contains each of the original training examples K times where $P(K = k)$ follows a binomial distribution:

$$P(K = k) = \binom{n}{k} p^k (1-p)^{n-k} = \binom{n}{k} \frac{1}{n}^k \left(1 - \frac{1}{n}\right)^{n-k}$$

This binomial distribution for large values of n tends to a Poisson(1) distribution, where Poisson(1)= $\exp(-1)/k!$. Using this fact, Oza and Russell [13, 14] proposed *Online Bagging*, an online method that instead of sampling with replacement, gives each example a weight according to Poisson(1). Figure 4 shows the pseudocode of this ensemble method.

ONLINE BAGGING(M)

    Input: M - number of classifiers in the ensemble

1   Initialize base models h_m for all $m \in \{1, 2, ..., M\}$
2   **for** each example (x, y) in Stream
3   **do for** $m = 1, 2, ..., M$
4   **do** Set $w = Poisson(1)$
5   Update h_m with the current example with weight w

6   **anytime output:**
7   **return** hypothesis: $h_{fin}(x) = \arg\max_{y \in Y} \sum_{t=1}^{T} I(h_t(x) = y)$

Fig. 4. Oza and Russell's *Online Bagging* for M models.

Example 1. Let D be a dataset of 4 instances : A, B, C, D. Imagine that we have 5 classifiers, and we run a non-streaming bagging, performing sampling with replacement. The inputs for each classifier will be the following:

Classifier 1: B, A, C, B
Classifier 2: D, B, A, D
Classifier 3: B, A, C, B
Classifier 4: B, C, B, B
Classifier 5: D, C, A, C

And this is equivalent to the following sorted inputs:

Classifier 1: A, B, B, C: A(1) B(2) C(1) D(0)
Classifier 2: A, B, D, D: A(1) B(1) C(0) D(2)
Classifier 3: A, B, B, C: A(1) B(2) C(1) D(0)
Classifier 4: B, B, B, C: A(0) B(3) C(1) D(0)
Classifier 5: A, C, C, D: A(1) B(0) C(2) D(1)

So, to perform bagging in a data streaming setting, we just need to assign each new instance that arrives a weight of Poisson(1).

When data is evolving over time, it is important that models adapt to the changes in the stream and evolve over time. `ADWIN` bagging [15] is the online bagging method of Oza and Russell with the addition of the `ADWIN` algorithm as a change detector and as an estimator for the weights of the boosting method. When a change is detected, the worst classifier of the ensemble of classifiers is removed and a new classifier is added to the ensemble.

A more powerful adaptive bagging exists that extends `ADWIN` bagging, called *leveraging bagging* [16]. It leverages the performance of bagging, with two randomization improvements: increasing resampling and using output detection codes. Figure 5 shows the pseudocode of this method.

LEVERAGING BAGGING(M)

Input: M - number of classifiers in the ensemble

1 Initialize base models h_m for all $m \in \{1, 2, ..., M\}$
2 Compute for each classifier m and class y a binary output
   code matrix $\mu_m(y)$
3 **for** each example (x, y) in Stream
4   **do for** $m = 1, 2, ..., M$
5   **do** Set $w = Poisson(\lambda)$
6   Update h_m with the current example
                 with weight w and binary mapped class $\mu_m(y)$
7   **if** `ADWIN` detects change in error of one of the classifiers
8   **then** Replace classifier with higher error with a new one

9 **anytime output:**
10 **return** hypothesis: $h_{fin}(x) = \arg\max_{y \in Y} \sum_{t=1}^{T} I(h_t(x) = \mu_t(y))$

Fig. 5. *Leveraging Bagging* for M models.

Resampling with replacement is done in Online Bagging using Poisson(1). There are other sampling mechanisms:

- Lee and Clyde [17] uses the Gamma distribution (Gamma(1,1)) to obtain a Bayesian version of Bagging. Note that Gamma(1,1) is equal to Exp(1).
- Bulhman and Yu [18] propose subagging, using resampling without replacement.

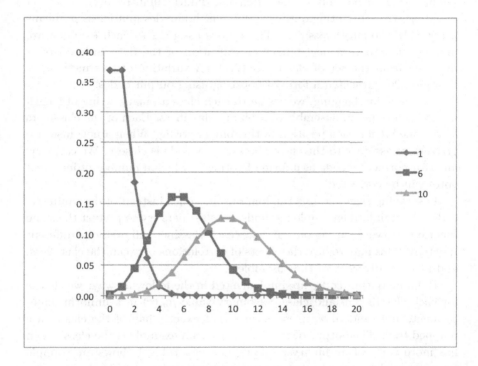

Fig. 6.   Poisson distribution.

Leveraging bagging increases the weights of this resampling using a larger value λ to compute the value of the Poisson distribution. The Poisson distribution is used to model the number of events occurring within a given time interval.

Figure 6 shows the probability function mass of the distribution of Poisson for several values of λ. The mean and variance of a Poisson distribution is λ. For $\lambda = 1$ we see that 37% of the values are zero, 37% are one, and 26%

are values greater than one. Using a weight of Poisson(1) we are taking out 37% of the examples, and repeating 26% of the examples, in a similar way to non streaming bagging. For $\lambda = 6$ we see that 0.25% of the values are zero, 45% are lower than six, 16% are six, and 39% are values greater than six. Using a value of $\lambda > 1$ for Poisson(λ) we are increasing the diversity of the weights and modifying the input space of the classifiers inside the ensemble. However, the optimal value of λ may be different for each dataset.

A second improvement is to add randomization at the output of the ensemble using output codes. Dieterich and Bakiri [19] introduced a method based on error-correcting output codes, which handles multiclass problems using only a binary classifier. The classes assigned to each example are modified to create a new binary classification of the data induced by a mapping from the set of classes to {0,1}. A variation of this method by Schapire [20] presented a form of boosting using output codes.

In leveraging bagging, we assign to each class a binary string of length n and then build an ensemble of n binary classifiers. Each of the classifiers learns one bit for each position in this binary string. When a new instance arrives, we assign x to the class whose binary code is closest. We can view an error-correcting code as a form of voting in which a number of incorrect votes can be corrected.

Leveraging bagging uses random output codes instead of deterministic codes. In standard ensemble methods, all classifiers try to predict the same function. However, using output codes each classifier will predict a different function. This may reduce the effects of correlations between the classifiers, and increase diversity of the ensemble.

Random output codes are implemented in the following way: we choose for each classifier m and class c a binary value $\mu_m(c)$ in a uniform, independent, and random way. We ensure that exactly half of the classes are mapped to 0. The output of the classifier for an example is the class which has more votes of its binary mapping classes. Table 1 shows an example for an ensemble of 6 classifiers in a classification task of 3 classes.

Leveraging bagging is an extension of ADWIN bagging and uses the same strategy to deal with concept drift. Algorithm 5 shows the pseudo-code for Leveraging Bagging. First it builds a matrix with the values of μ for each classifier and class. For each new instance that arrives, it gives it a random weight of $Poisson(k)$. It trains the classifier with this weight, and when a change is detected, the worst classifier of the ensemble of classifiers is removed and a new classifier is added to the ensemble. To predict the class of an example, it computes for each class c the sum of the votes for $\mu(c)$ of

Table 1.   Example matrix of random output
codes for 3 classes and 6 classifiers.

	Class 1	Class 2	Class 3
Classifier 1	0	0	1
Classifier 2	0	1	1
Classifier 3	1	0	0
Classifier 4	1	1	0
Classifier 5	1	0	1
Classifier 6	0	1	0

all the ensemble classifiers, and outputs as a prediction the class with the most votes.

3.3. *Classification in MOA*

MOA contains stream generators, classifiers and evaluation methods. Figure 7 shows the MOA graphical user interface. However, a command line interface is also available.

Considering data streams as data generated from pure distributions, MOA models a concept drift event as a weighted combination of two pure distributions that characterizes the target concepts before and after the drift. Within the framework, it is possible to define the probability that instances of the stream belong to the new concept after the drift. It uses the sigmoid function, as an elegant and practical solution [15, 21].

MOA contains the data generators most commonly found in the literature. MOA streams can be built using generators, reading ARFF files, joining several streams, or filtering streams. They allow for the simulation of a potentially infinite sequence of data. The following generators are currently available: Random Tree Generator, SEA Concepts Generator, STAGGER Concepts Generator, Rotating Hyperplane, Random RBF Generator, LED Generator, Waveform Generator, and Function Generator.

MOA contains several classifier methods such as: Naive Bayes, Decision Stump, Hoeffding Tree, Hoeffding Adaptive Tree [11], Hoeffding Option Tree [22], Bagging, Boosting, Bagging using ADWIN, Bagging using Adaptive-Size Hoeffding Trees [15] and Leveraging Bagging [16].

For example, a non-trivial example of the EvaluateInterleavedTestThenTrain task creating a comma separated values file, training the HoeffdingTree classifier on the WaveformGenerator data, training and testing on a total of 100 million examples, and testing every one million examples, is encapsulated by the following command line:

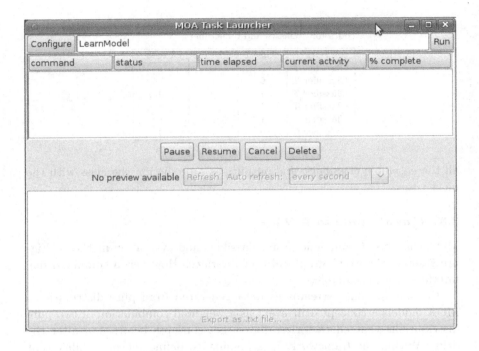

Fig. 7.   MOA graphical user interface.

```
java -cp.:moa.jar:weka.jar -javaagent:sizeofag.jar moa.DoTask\
  "EvaluateInterleavedTestThenTrain -l HoeffdingTree \
  -s generators.WaveformGenerator \
  -i 100000000 -f 1000000" > htresult.csv
```

MOA is easy to use and extend. A simple approach to writing a new classifier is to extend moa.classifiers.AbstractClassifier, which will take care of certain details to ease the task.

4. Clustering

Clustering is an *unsupervised* learning task that mines unlabeled data. It is useful, when we have unlabeled data, and we want to find relevant groups in the data. Clustering consists in the distribution of a set of instances into non-known groups according to some common relations or affinities. The main difference with classification is that the groups are not-known before starting the learning process. There are many examples of clustering:

market segmentation of customers, or finding social network communities are two examples.

We can see clustering as an optimization problem, where we want to optimize a cost function. Some clustering methods needs the k parameter to know the quantity of clusters to find in the data, and other methods does not have any restriction in the number of clusters to find in the data.

The k-means clustering method is one of the most used methods in clustering, due to its simplicity. The k-means algorithm starts selecting k centroids in a random way. After that there are two main steps: first assign to each instance the nearest point, and second, recompute the cluster centroids using these new assignments. This is done in a iterative way, until a stopping criterion is accomplished, mainly based in the sum of the distance to the centroids. k-means is not a streaming method as it requires to do several passes over the data.

Streaming methods for clustering have two phases, an on-line and an off-line phase. In the on-line, a set of micro-clusters is computed and updated in a very fast way, and in the off-line phase, a classical batch clustering method as k-means is performed using the micro-clusters computed in the on-line phase. The on-line phase is doing only one pass over the data, and the off-line phase is doing several passes, but not over all the data, only over the set of micro-clusters, usually a small set of less than 200 points.

4.1. *Clustering in MOA*

MOA contains also an experimental framework for clustering data streams, so that it will be easy for researchers to run experimental data stream benchmarks. The features of MOA for stream clustering are:

- data generators for evolving data streams (including events such as novelty, merge, etc. [23]),
- an extensible set of stream clustering algorithms,
- evaluation measures for stream clustering,
- visualization tools for analyzing results and comparing different settings.

For stream clustering we added new data generators that support the simulation of cluster evolution events such as merging or disappearing of clusters [23].

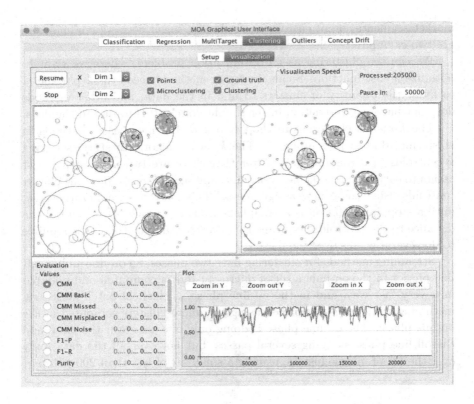

Fig. 8.   Visualization tab of the clustering MOA graphical user interface.

MOA contains several stream clustering algorithms such as the following ones:

- StreamKM++ [24]: It computes a small weighted sample of the data stream and it uses the k-means++ algorithm as a randomized seeding technique to choose the first values for the clusters. To compute the small sample, it employs coreset constructions using a coreset tree for speed up.

- CluStream [25]: It maintains statistical information about the data using micro-clusters. These micro-clusters are temporal extensions of cluster feature vectors. The micro-clusters are stored at snapshots in time following a pyramidal pattern. This pattern allows to recall summary statistics from different time horizons.

- ClusTree [26]: It is a parameter free algorithm automatically adapting to the speed of the stream and it is capable of detecting concept drift, novelty, and outliers in the stream. It uses a compact and self-adaptive index structure for maintaining stream summaries.

- Den-Stream [27]: It uses dense micro-clusters (named core-micro-cluster) to summarize clusters. To maintain and distinguish the potential clusters and outliers, this method presents core-micro-cluster and outlier micro-cluster structures.

- D-Stream [28]: This method maps each input data record into a grid and it computes the grid density. The grids are clustered based on the density. This algorithm adopts a density decaying technique to capture the dynamic changes of a data stream.

- CobWeb [29]. One of the first incremental methods for clustering data. It uses a classification tree. Each node in a classification tree represents a class (concept) and is labeled by a probabilistic concept that summarizes the attribute-value distributions of objects classified under the node.

MOA contains measures for analyzing the performance of the clustering models generated. It contains measures commonly used in the literature as well as novel evaluation measures to compare and evaluate both online and offline components. The available measures evaluate both the correct assignment of examples [30] and the compactness of the resulting clustering. The visualization component (cf. Figures 8 and 9) allows to visualize the stream as well as the clustering results, choose dimensions for multi dimensional settings, and compare experiments with different settings in parallel.

Beside providing an evaluation framework, the second key objective is the extensibility of the benchmark suite regarding the set of implemented algorithms as well as the available data feeds and evaluation measures.

Figure 8 shows a screenshot of our visualization tab. For this screenshot two different settings of the CluStream algorithm [25] were compared on the same stream setting (including merge/split events every 50000 examples) and five measures were chosen for online evaluation (CMD, F1, Precision, Recall and SSQ). The upper part of the GUI offers options to pause and resume the stream, adjust the visualization speed, choose the dimensions for x and y as well as the components to be displayed (points, micro- and macro clustering and ground truth). The lower part of the GUI displays the measured values for both settings as numbers (left side, including mean values) and the currently selected measure as a plot over the arrived examples (right, F1 measure in this example). For the given setting one can see a clear drop in the performance after the split event at roughly

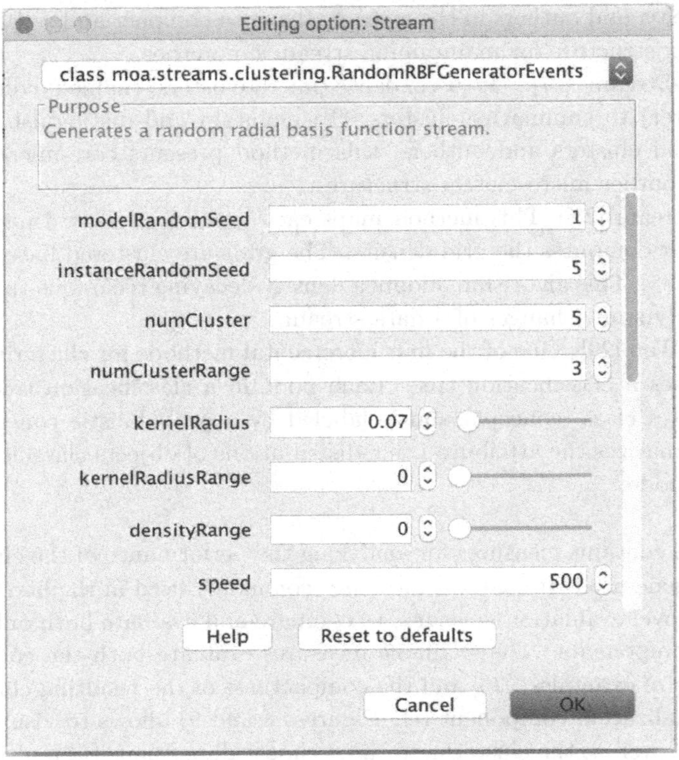

Fig. 9. Option dialog for the RBF data generator (by storing and loading settings benchmark streaming data sets can be shared for repeatability and comparison).

160000 examples (event details are shown when choosing the corresponding vertical line in the plot). While this holds for both settings, the left configuration (red, CluStream with 100 micro clusters) is constantly outperformed by the right configuration (blue, CluStream with 20 micro clusters).

5. Conclusions

MOA is a classification and clustering system for massive data streams with the following characteristics:

- benchmark streaming data sets through stored, shared, and repeatable settings for the various data feeds and noise options, both synthetic and real,

- set of implemented algorithms for comparison to approaches from the literature,
- open source tool and framework for research and teaching similar to WEKA.

MOA is written in Java. The main benefits of Java are portability, where applications can be run on any platform with an appropriate Java virtual machine, and the strong and well-developed support libraries. Use of the language is widespread, and features such as the automatic garbage collection help to reduce programmer burden and error.

MOA can be found at:

http://moa.cms.waikato.ac.nz/

The website includes a tutorial, an API reference, a user manual, and a manual about mining data streams. Several examples of how the software can be used are available. The sources are publicly available and are released under the GNU GPL license.

The core team and the community developers of MOA plan to continue extending MOA by adding more classification methods, outlier detection, multi-label and multi-target learning, and frequent pattern mining methods.

References

[1] R. Kirkby. *Improving Hoeffding Trees*. PhD thesis, University of Waikato (November, 2007).

[2] E. S. Page, Continuous inspection schemes, *Biometrika.* **41**(1/2), 100–115 (1954).

[3] J. Gama, P. Medas, G. Castillo, and P. Rodrigues. Learning with drift detection. In *SBIA Brazilian Symposium on Artificial Intelligence*, pp. 286–295 (2004).

[4] A. Bifet and R. Gavaldà. Learning from time-changing data with adaptive windowing. In *SIAM International Conference on Data Mining* (2007).

[5] M. Datar, A. Gionis, P. Indyk, and R. Motwani, Maintaining stream statistics over sliding windows, *SIAM Journal on Computing.* **14**(1), 27–45 (2002).

[6] J. Gama, R. Sebastião, and P. P. Rodrigues. Issues in evaluation of stream learning algorithms. In *Proceedings of the 15th ACM SIGKDD International Conference on Knowledge Discovery and Data Mining*, pp. 329–338 (2009).

[7] A. Bifet, G. D. F. Morales, J. Read, G. Holmes, and B. Pfahringer. Efficient online evaluation of big data stream classifiers. In *Proceedings of the 21th ACM SIGKDD International Conference on Knowledge Discovery and Data Mining, Sydney, NSW, Australia, August 10–13, 2015*, pp. 59–68 (2015).

[8] P. Domingos and G. Hulten. Mining high-speed data streams. In *Proceedings of the 6th ACM SIGKDD International Conference on Knowledge Discovery and Data Mining*, pp. 71–80 (2000).

[9] J. Gama and P. Medas, Learning decision trees from dynamic data streams, *Journal of Universal Computer Science*, **11**(8), 1353–1366 (2005).

[10] G. Holmes, R. Kirkby, and B. Pfahringer. Stress-testing hoeffding trees. In *PKDD*, pp. 495–502 (2005).

[11] A. Bifet and R. Gavaldà. Adaptive learning from evolving data streams. In *8th International Symposium on Intelligent Data Analysis*, pp. 249–260 (2009).

[12] L. Breiman, Bagging predictors, *Machine Learning*, **24**(2), 123–140 (1996). ISSN 0885-6125.

[13] N. C. Oza and S. J. Russell. Experimental comparisons of online and batch versions of bagging and boosting. In *KDD*, pp. 359–364 (2001).

[14] N. Oza and S. Russell. Online bagging and boosting. In *Artificial Intelligence and Statistics 2001*, pp. 105–112, Morgan Kaufmann (2001).

[15] A. Bifet, G. Holmes, B. Pfahringer, R. Kirkby, and R. Gavaldà. New ensemble methods for evolving data streams. In *15th ACM SIGKDD International Conference on Knowledge Discovery and Data Mining* (2009).

[16] A. Bifet, G. Holmes, and B. Pfahringer. Leveraging bagging for evolving data streams. In *ECML/PKDD (1)*, pp. 135–150 (2010).

[17] H. K. H. Lee and M. A. Clyde, Lossless online bayesian bagging, *Journal of Machine Learning Research*, **5**, 143–151 (2004). ISSN 1532-4435.

[18] P. Bühlmann and B. Yu, Analyzing bagging, *Annals of Statistics* (2003).

[19] T. G. Dietterich and G. Bakiri, Solving multiclass learning problems via error-correcting output codes, *Journal of Artificial Intelligence Research (JAIR)*, **2**, 263–286 (1995).

[20] R. E. Schapire. Using output codes to boost multiclass learning problems. In *ICML '97: Proceedings of the Fourteenth International Conference on Machine Learning*, pp. 313–321, Morgan Kaufmann Publishers Inc., San Francisco, CA, USA (1997). ISBN 1-55860-486-3.

[21] A. Bifet, G. Holmes, B. Pfahringer, and R. Gavaldà. Improving adaptive bagging methods for evolving data streams. In *First Asian Conference on Machine Learning, ACML 2009* (2009).

[22] B. Pfahringer, G. Holmes, and R. Kirkby. Handling numeric attributes in hoeffding trees. In *PAKDD Pacific-Asia Conference on Knowledge Discovery and Data Mining*, pp. 296–307 (2008).

[23] M. Spiliopoulou, I. Ntoutsi, Y. Theodoridis, and R. Schult. MONIC: modeling and monitoring cluster transitions. In *ACM KDD*, pp. 706–711 (2006).

[24] M. R. Ackermann, C. Lammersen, M. Märtens, C. Raupach, C. Sohler, and K. Swierkot. StreamKM++: A clustering algorithm for data streams. In *SIAM ALENEX* (2010).

[25] C. C. Aggarwal, J. Han, J. Wang, and P. S. Yu. A framework for clustering evolving data streams. In *VLDB*, pp. 81–92 (2003).

[26] P. Kranen, I. Assent, C. Baldauf, and T. Seidl. The ClusTree: indexing micro-clusters for anytime stream mining. *Knowledge and information systems*, **29**(2), 249–272 (2011).

[27] F. Cao, M. Ester, W. Qian, and A. Zhou. Density-based clustering over an evolving data stream with noise. In *SDM* (2006).

[28] L. Tu and Y. Chen, Stream data clustering based on grid density and attraction, *ACM Transactions on Knowledge Discovery from Data*, **3**(3), 1–27 (2009). ISSN 1556-4681. doi: http://doi.acm.org/10.1145/1552303.1552305.

[29] D. H. Fisher, Knowledge acquisition via incremental conceptual clustering, *Machine Learning*, **2**(2), 139–172 (1987). ISSN 0885-6125. doi: http://dx.doi.org/10.1023/A:1022852608280.

[30] J. Chen. Adapting the right measures for k-means clustering. In *ACM KDD*, pp. 877–884 (2009).

Chapter 2

Weightless Neural Modeling for Mining Data Streams

Douglas O. Cardoso[*,§], João Gama[†,¶] and Felipe França[‡,‖]

*Centro Federal de Educação Tecnológica Celso Suckow da Fonseca
Petrópolis, RJ, Brazil
§douglas.cardoso@cefet-rj.br

†Universidade do Porto, LIAAD-INESC TEC
Oporto, Portugal
¶jgama@fep.up.pt

‡Universidade Federal do Rio de Janeiro, PESC-COPPE
Rio de Janeiro, RJ, Brazil
‖felipe@cos.ufrj.br

Learning from data streams can only be realized by systems which are not only effective but also efficient. That is, knowledge discovery in this context is impossible without being aware of the computational resources available. Weightless artificial neural networks (WANNs) are based on an alternative principle to iterative optimization of weights employed by most mainstream artificial neural network models and related tools. WANNs explicitly manage knowledge pieces, which are stored by RAM nodes. Such foundational difference reflects on the adaptability of these models to streaming inputs: in such scenario, the application of weightless models can be considered more natural than the same for their weighted counterparts, with an ample control over learning capability as well as resources consumption. This chapter details a WANN-based approach for mining data streams, which allows the maintenance of an up-to-date data summary which can be used for several purposes. The insights and original ideas which power such model are explained as well, enabling novel applications and further development of them.

1. Introduction

Because of technological facts of our time as social networks, Internet of Things, ubiquitous sensing and others, data generation processes became faster and more numerous, while also acting as unbounded data sources. In order to extract knowledge from such data, using classic machine learning methods to process a data sample is possible. However, as fast as more data is generated, knowledge previously obtained becomes obsolete. In this scenario, classical methods could learn from scratch every time a new batch of observations becomes available. Unfortunately, this strategy has some weaknesses:[1]

- it can be hard to decide how large these batches should be;
- if the batches are too small, the lack of training data could harm the learning process;
- on the other hand, if they are too large, they may feature concept drift which could also have a negative effect on learning;
- learning from scratch can be very time consuming, what may not be compatible with data input rate.

In the context being considered, data temporality is a key concept. However, classical machine learning and data mining techniques do not take such aspect into account. This explains why their application in this case would expectedly fail. Hence, instead of approaching such learning task considering as input a sequence of data sets, using a single data stream in the same regard is the better alternative. This implies processing temporal data as it is, and not as if such time dimension was not present. Consequently, this also implies moving away from classical learning tools and relying on true stream-oriented methods, which would uninterruptedly extract up-to-date information from data. This way, data processing is realized with a greater granularity and responsiveness to changes in the underlying data distribution.

Methods developed to deal with data streams should meet efficiency constraints imposed by the characteristics of their data sources:[2] input data is assumed to be infinitely large, so that it should be processed incrementally instead of as a single batch; because data input rates can be very high, buffering observations unrestrictedly is forbidden; as a scalability requirement, the computational cost of processing a single observation should not be related to the number of observations already processed. The observation of such requirements led to the development of data stream mining systems which are not only effective with respect to knowledge extraction, but they are also fast enough to be scalable as desired.[3] Moreover, these systems also employ efficient memory management policies, usually based on sampling or summarization techniques.[4]

Considering these challenges,[5] Wilkes, Stonham and Aleksander Recognition Device (WiSARD) was brought into play as powerful, flexible, multi-purpose learner. This artificial neural network (ANN) model provides the means for pattern recognition working as a lazy learner, memorizing and matching small information pieces extracted from its inputs. The original and most frequent use of this model is standard classification. However, it has been used for other tasks: unsupervised learning,[6,7] rule induction,[8] generative modeling[9] and natural language processing[10,11] are some recent examples of these applications. Such flexibility inspired the idea of exploring its adaptation to feed from streaming data. It was also considered that this could enable to reproduce its previous uses in such new and increasingly popular scenario.

Other interesting characteristics of this model for the intended development include its native high-speed functioning, which does not rely on iterative optimization of any form. Instead, learning is realized recording the occurrence of values obtained from randomly mapping the training observations to a high-dimensional binary feature space. This way, each observation is processed individually, and learning is not affected by the input order of observations in a training set. Moreover, learning and recognition can be interleaved with no restriction. Such high-level granularity and stability could enable proper learning even if concept drift happens, responding to such events in a reasonable way. Moreover, the explicit memorization architecture of this model allows a fine control over its space complexity, what is crucial to handle possibly large volumes of streaming data. It is also valid to notice that most ANN models lack these characteristics, what supports choosing WiSARD over other options.

In order to accomplish the targeted stream-oriented learning process, it was considered necessary to change two aspects of WiSARD functioning. The first of these aspects regards decremental learning. That is, since data is continuously flowing, this model should incrementally learn from the most recent observations while outdated knowledge is discarded. Disposing expired information is important not only because of efficiency, since storage is limited while data is not. Besides this, there is no point in maintaining knowledge that is not up-to-date, which could be mistaken as current, hurting model predictive capabilities. The second aspects is WiSARD defective operation when dealing with unbalanced data collections. It is impossible to guarantee that during the entire stream processing there would be a similar number of examples of all classes to be learned. Thus, it would be necessary to enable proper learning even under this unfavorable condition. This chapter presents ideas to address these two points.

This is the outline of the remaining sections: Section 2 presents the WiSARD model, detailing its functioning, how it was inspired and comparing its functioning to other well known statistical and machine learning tools; Section 3 describes how decremental learning could be accomplished while preserving the characteristics of the base learner; Section 4 details a countermeasure to data imbalance with minimum impact on WiSARD algorithmic complexity; Section 5 presents an application of the proposed framework for clustering; at last, some concluding remarks are provided in Section 6.

2. The WiSARD Model

Artificial neural networks are statistical tools whose design was inspired by nervous systems of living beings, created to emulate some of the learning capability of their biological counterparts. There exists a great variety of ANN models, which have different characteristics and are used for several purposes: function approximation, signal processing, classification, clustering, time series prediction and others. But all these models share a basic design principle: each of them is defined as a collection of units, called nodes or neurons, which are combined according to the model definition, working collectively.

Biological neurons operate as signal processing units: they receive stimuli through its dendrites, which are organized as a tree; these stimuli are combined during the traversal of the dendritic tree; resulting signals of such combination reach the soma, where a response for such inputs is generated; this response is forwarded trough the axon to muscles, glands or other neurons whose dendrites are connected to this axon by synapses. Figure 1 illustrates these components of a generic neuron.

The most popular mathematical abstraction of biological neurons was originally proposed by McCulloch and Pitts.[12] In such model, the synapses are substituted by edges, connecting the nodes of the neural network. The stimuli the neuron receives is substituted by the input of numerical values. These values are multiplied by numerical weights associated to the edges they traverse. At last, the sum of these multiplications is input to some function, whose outcome is used as the output of the neuron. Such

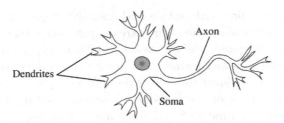

Figure 1: A sketch of a biological neuron.[a]

modeling is reasonable from both biological and mathematical points of view. Various ANN models rely on the modification of weights of its edges by the superposition of the effects of the observations which compose the training sample.

Weightless ANNs [13] are memory-based alternatives to weights-based ones. All links of these networks have no weight, acting as the simplest communication channels, exercising no effect on data traffic. Therefore, their nodes are responsible for the learning capability these networks exhibit. These nodes operate as memory units, keeping small portions of information, which are combined when a query regarding the knowledge the system possess needs to be answered. These information pieces are the outcome of mapping the data used as knowledge source.

The biological inspiration of these nodes is the influence of dendritic trees on neuron functioning. In the first abstraction described, such trees were modeled as a weighted edges, which multiply the neuron inputs before the application of the activation function on their summation. Although practical, this is a rough simplification of how these trees operate. As a matter of fact, the input signals of biological neurons, which can be of two types (excitatory or inhibitory), are combined by the dendritic tree before reaching the neuron soma, where they prompt the generation of a new signal. This action can be naturally compared to the definition of a boolean key used to access a index of boolean values. In fact, this is how the most basic neurons of weightless ANN models work.

The WiSARD[5] is a weightless ANN. The way it works is quite simple: it implements a mapping-and-memorization scheme in a collection of nodes organized in a single layer; the outputs these nodes can provide are limited to 0 or 1; these outputs are aggregated through ordinary summation.

For classification, this model provides for each class a value in the interval $[0, 1]$, representing how well the provided observation matches the acquired knowledge regarding the classes. For binary classification, it is straightforward to transform a two-values answer provided by WiSARD to a single value as an output from a Multilayer Perceptron: the subtraction of the two given values is enough for this. However, the answer format of WiSARD is more informative: for example, a small difference between two values close to 1 possibly is an evidence that both classes could be the true class of the input observation; but the same difference between values close to 0 could be an evidence that none of the classes are good guesses.

The values which compose an answer obtained from WiSARD are computed from structures called discriminators. Each discriminator is responsible for storing the knowledge regarding a class, as well as assessing the matching between the class it represents and any observation whose true class has to be predicted. How a discriminator learns about its respective class is described in Algorithm 1. In a sentence, it records in its nodes the values resulting from mapping the observations in the training sample. Mind some notation introduced here: the discriminator of class $\dot{y}$ is represented by $\Delta_{\dot{y}}$; the jth node of $\Delta_{\dot{y}}$ is represented by $\Delta_{\dot{y},j}$; the number of nodes which compose each discriminator is represented by δ.

1: **for all** $\Delta_{\dot{y},j}$, the network nodes **do**

2:      $\Delta_{\dot{y},j} \leftarrow \varnothing$ ▷ All nodes operate as sets, and are initially empty

3: **for all** pairs $(\vec{x}_i, y_i)$, the training sample **do**

4:      Let addressing$(\vec{x}_i) = (a_1\ a_2\ \cdots\ a_\delta)$ be a vector mapped from $\vec{x}_i$

5:      **for all** addresses a_j in addressing$(\vec{x}_i)$ **do**

6:          $\Delta_{y_i,j} \leftarrow \Delta_{y_i,j} \cup \{a_j\}$ ▷ Adding address a_j to node $\Delta_{y_i,j}$

Algorithm 1: A description of WiSARD training procedure.

There are several analogies between hardware systems and WiSARD. Consequently, some parts of its structure are named using terms which belong to this domain. For example, its nodes are called RAM nodes, a direct reference to their memory-like operation, different from the functional nodes of the weights-based networks. Like physical RAM modules, their content is retrieved or altered using addresses, defined by an *addressing* procedure. Despite this nomenclature, RAM nodes work identically to sets, well-known mathematical structures, and are commonly implemented using hash tables. Likewise, addresses can be seen as habitual vectors, obtained from mapping the observations.

After training, a WiSARD instance can rate the matching between any known class $\hat{y}$ and an observation $\vec{x}$ as shown in Expression (1a). At last, an observation $\vec{x}$ is classified according to Expression (1b).

$$\text{matching}(\vec{x}, \hat{y}) = \frac{1}{\delta} \sum_i \mathbf{1}_{\Delta_{\hat{y}, i}}(\text{addressing}_i(\vec{x}))^{\text{b}}; \tag{1a}$$

$$\hat{y} = \underset{\hat{y}}{\text{argmax}} \ \text{matching}(\vec{x}, \hat{y}). \tag{1b}$$

There is an extra level of generalization implied by the matching computation. Consider that a discriminator Δ_+ was trained using the observations of a set $X_+ = \{\ldots, \vec{x}_i, \ldots\}$. For a given observation $\vec{x}$, Expression (2) holds: $\vec{x}$ perfectly matches Δ_+ (i.e., $\text{matching}(\vec{x}, +) = 1$) iff all addresses of $\vec{x}$ match addresses of observations in X_+. Thus, the combination of addresses obtained from different observations allow the recognition of observations which do not belong to the training sample.

$$\forall_i, \exists_{\vec{x}' \in X_+} \ \text{addressing}_i(\vec{x}') = \text{addressing}_i(\vec{x}) \iff \text{matching}(\vec{x}, +) = 1. \tag{2}$$

Mathematically, WiSARD addressing procedure can be described as a composite function $g \circ f : \mathbb{R}^n \to \{0, 1\}^{\delta \times \beta}$, such that:

- $f : \mathbb{R}^n \to \{0, 1\}^{n \times \gamma}$ is any encoding function[14,15] which provides binary representations of the observations;
- $g : \{0, 1\}^{n \times \gamma} \to \{0, 1\}^{\delta \times \beta}$ is a random mapping defined prior to training, described as $\vec{A} \mapsto \vec{B}, B_{i,j} = A_{i',j'}$, for arbitrary i, j, i', j'.

Variable γ, which controls encoding resolution, and β, the length of the addresses, are model parameters. If data is originally binary, an identity-like function can be used for encoding: that is the case for black-and-white images, the kind of data for which WiSARD was originally developed. Otherwise, for example, if all data features are scaled to interval $[0, 1]$, the zero-padded-unary encoding function, Expression (3a), can be used.

$$f(\vec{x}) = (h(x_0), h(x_1), \cdots, h(x_n)), \tag{3a}$$

$$h(y) = ([\lfloor \gamma y \rceil \geq 1], [\lfloor \gamma y \rceil \geq 2], \cdots, [\lfloor \gamma y \rceil \geq \gamma])^{\text{c}}. \tag{3b}$$

---

[b]The indicator function: $\mathbf{1}_A(x) = 1$ if $x \in A$; otherwise, $\mathbf{1}_A(x) = 0$.
[c]$\lfloor x \rceil$ represents the nearest integer of real number x.

For a training sample X, the time complexity of WiSARD training procedure, Algorithm 1, is $O(|X|\,\delta\,\beta)$. That is, for each of the $|X|$ observations, δ node updates are realized, and the cost of each of these updates can be conservatively equated to the definition of a key of β bits. It can be noticed that there is no dependence between such cost and the dimensionality of the observations. However, this dependence can be established according to how addressing is performed. In turn, a single prediction according to Expression (1b) requires $O(|\dot{Y}|\,\delta\,\beta)$ steps, where $|\dot{Y}|$ represents the number of known classes.

The discriminator nodes register the occurrence of addresses which are β-bits strings. There are 2^β possible values for these strings. This can be used to asymptotically define the memory complexity of a WiSARD discriminator: $O(\delta\,\beta\,2^\beta)$. This bound can be considered too "pessimist", since it is quite uncommon for a node to register $O(2^\beta)$ addresses: first, such condition presumes that $|X| \geq O(2^\beta)$, while in commonly used WiSARD setups, $|X| \ll 2^\beta$; second, it also presumes that the number of distinct addresses to be obtained from observations in X will be of the order of 2^β, but this is hardly feasible, because in practice observations input to the same discriminator, as examples of a given class, are expected to have addresses in common. A better bound, although still very conservative, is $O(|X|\,\delta\,\beta)$.

3. Decremental Learning

As originally defined, an instance of the WiSARD model would be able to gradually process a data stream: this comes from the fact that WiSARD training is performed incrementally. However, based on such feature, the content of its nodes could be expanded up to the point of saturation.[9] That is, the pattern the discriminator represents would become too general, making recognition meaningless. In order to avoid reaching such undesirable condition, discarding stored addresses which are no longer useful is necessary. In this sense, such usefulness should be defined according to data temporality: an address needs to be kept as long as it contributes to the representation of current knowledge. Such contribution can be verified by occurrence of some observation which also provides this already stored address. Consequently, it becomes necessary to register how recently each address was matched, so that their disposal could happen based on such record.

The most straightforward way to implement this idea is to consider the existence of a dictionary D, which maps addresses to time stamps. As some incoming observation $\vec{x}$ is processed on instant t, this dictionary is updated as follows: $D_{j,a_j} \leftarrow t$, for each component a_j of addressing$(\vec{x}) = (a_1 \ a_2 \ \cdots \ a_\delta)$. Including this operation in WiSARD training procedure does not alter the computational complexity of the model, since it represents a constant increase of its time and space costs. This way, on every instant during stream processing, each stored address would be related to a time stamp representing its recency.

Despite such modification, no address would be discarded since it was not defined the criteria to rule an address as outdated. A simple criteria is to consider as expired any address whose respective time stamp is below some given threshold. Such threshold should be updated while the stream is processed: otherwise, it would become useless as the values of the time stamps increase over time. An idea in this regard is to assume that at instant t, this threshold is $t - \omega$, where ω is an additional model parameter. Such idea can be directly related to the sliding window aging model,[16] so that the window length is ω. This way, whenever $D_{j,a_j} < t - \omega$ for any pair (j, a_j), each discriminator $\dot{y}$ should be updated as follows: $\Delta_{\dot{y},j} \leftarrow \Delta_{\dot{y},j} \setminus \{a_j\}$.

After deciding how outdated addresses are ruled as so, trying to identify these elements among all others is naturally the next step. A naive approach for this is to verify the expiration status of all entries of the dictionary D, one by one. Such action would be prohibitively expensive, as it can be compared to processing each of the ω observations in the sliding window once again, and should be performed every time an novel observation is received. A better strategy is to consider D a least recently used (LRU) dictionary, so that its entries are sorted based on how recently they were updated. This reduces to a minimum the cost of determining which entry of D should be first considered for disposal. Although the cost of maintaining such structure is not negligible, it is indisputably more efficient than the aforementioned naive approach. The combination of the ideas just described represent one solution for the accomplishment of decremental learning by WiSARD, as shown in Algorithm 2.

One possible variation of this given solution regards the substitution of sliding window threshold $t - \omega$ by the definition of the maximum number of elements of D. Therefore, whenever the number of entries of D reaches this maximum, adding a new entry requires discarding an existing one, as well as its respective RAM nodes addresses. This is an interesting alterna-

1: **for all** triples $(\vec{x}_i, y_i, t_i)$, the streaming observations **do**

2:     **while** min $D < t - \omega$ **do**

3:         $j, a_j = \underset{j, a_j}{\operatorname{argmin}}\ D_{j, a_j}$

4:         **for all** $\dot{y} \in \dot{Y}$ **do**

5:             $\Delta_{\dot{y}, j} \leftarrow \Delta_{\dot{y}, j} \setminus \{a_j\}$

6:         Delete D_{j, a_j}

7:     Let addressing$(\vec{x}_i) = (a_1\ a_2\ \cdots\ a_\delta)$ be a vector mapped from $\vec{x}_i$

8:     **for all** addresses a_j in addressing$(\vec{x}_i)$ **do**

9:         $\Delta_{y_i, j} \leftarrow \Delta_{y_i, j} \cup \{a_j\}$ ▷ Adding address a_j to node $\Delta_{y_i, j}$

10:         $D_{j, a_j} \leftarrow t$

Algorithm 2: A stream-oriented WiSARD training procedure.

tive to using a fixed-size window to decide about the disposal of outdated knowledge. Instead, limiting the number of elements in D leads to the implicit definition of an adaptive window. Such window becomes larger when input data is repetitive, what can represent stream stability, and shrinks otherwise. Furthermore, this allows setting a hard limit to memory usage, what can be useful in certain cases.

The can be variations of the original solution to learn decrementally. For example, instead of recording when an address was last matched, the dictionary D could register the last time the addresses were written. Consequently, instead of being indexed by pairs (j, a_j), the keys of D would be triples $(\dot{y}, j, a_j)$, in which $\dot{y}$ represents a discriminator. Treating each discriminator separately looks reasonable considering that the same pair (j, a_j) can contribute in very distinct ways to the up-to-date definitions of two different patterns. That is, in a given instant during stream processing, the triple $(\dot{y}, j, a_j)$ could be about to expire while $(\dot{y}', j, a_j)$ was just written. On the downside, depending on overlaps between patterns, this idea could be significantly more expensive with respect to space complexity.

4. Learning from Unbalanced Streams

For the targeted stream-oriented version of WiSARD, proper handling unbalanced data is as important as the efficient disposal of outdated knowl-

edge. That is, both aspects need to be considered in order to avoid saturation, a condition in which WiSARD learning and predictive capabilities
are nullified. With respect to data imbalance, saturation is a consequence
of the memorization-and-matching mechanism employed by this model, as
shown by the following reasoning:

(1) learning is realized storing binary features (i.e., addresses), while pat-
    tern recognition happens matching the stored addresses to those ob-
    tained from unlabeled observations;
(2) a pattern with numerous and varied examples has a greater chance of
    comprising a large collection of addresses;
(3) thus, it is more probable to relate an unlabeled observation to this
    pattern than to one with few training examples;
(4) in the worst case, any observation would be related to the pattern with
    most examples, whose respective discriminator would be saturated.

It is also interesting to notice that imbalance level can fluctuate during
the entire stream length, what represents an extra challenge in order to
solve this matter. A primitive attempt to counter imbalance while using
WiSARD for data streams mining[17] assumed that the chance of a discriminator to be saturated increases monotonically over time. However, because
learning happens not only incrementally but also decrementally, the collection of features comprised by a discriminator can become larger but can
also shrink during stream processing. Therefore, the ideal approach for
handling imbalance should be adaptive, based on the extent of the content
of each discriminator.[7]

Based on this reasoning, the *cardinality* of a discriminator is defined
as in Expression (4a). Still in this regard, Expression (4b) is called *normalized matching rate* and targets countering saturation considering the
cardinality in its computation. It can be noticed that the denominator
of matching$^*(k, \vec{x})$ is the geometric mean of the size of the nodes of Δ_k,
what is consistent with way the sets of addresses are combined for generalization and pattern recognition. Moreover, the cardinality of a discriminator is asymptotically equivalent to the area of the feature space itself

encompasses: $|\Delta_k| \sim \int \text{matching}(k, \vec{x}) \, d^n \vec{x}$.

$$|\Delta_k| = \left(\prod_j |\Delta_{k,j}| \right) ; \tag{4a}$$

$$\text{matching}^*(k, \vec{x}) = \frac{\text{matching}(k, \vec{x})}{(|\Delta_k|)^{1/\delta}}. \tag{4b}$$

Replacing the original matching rate with its just described normalized variant does not increase the computational complexity of the system. Therefore, there is no reason to avoid its use because of efficiency. This way, its adoption could only be rejected if this could have a negative effect on WiSARD predictive capability. Fortunately, it can be perceived that its participation on matching computation is equivalent to a regularization term, penalizing a discriminator according to how general, or vague is the pattern it represents. In this regard, the following example comes in handy: if $\text{matching}(\dot{y}, \vec{x}) = \text{matching}(\dot{y}', \vec{x})$ but $|\Delta_{\dot{y}}| > |\Delta_{\dot{y}'}|$, predicting that $\vec{x}$ is an example of the pattern represented by $\dot{y}'$ is sensible; after all, the pertinence to both discriminators is the same, despite the fact that $\dot{y}'$ is a more strict pattern; this way, even if $\text{matching}(\dot{y}, \vec{x}) > \text{matching}(\dot{y}', \vec{x})$ choosing $\dot{y}'$ over $\dot{y}$ could still be valid.

The perspective of the cardinality of a discriminator as a regularization term for normalized matching rate definition allows further developments. For example, consider that regularization terms are usually attached to some weighting factor. This fact can motivate the addition of a factor of such kind to WiSARD matching rate definition. Another reason for such modification is the additional flexibility provided by this parameter. That is, the influence of cardinality on matching computation can be more or less necessary, depending on the circumstances. After all, regular WiSARD provided interesting results despite not considering such participation at all. The outcome of this last reflection is Expression (5), named *adjusted matching rate*. Its calculation depends on an additional model parameter μ, the cardinality weight. Setting $\mu = 0$ reduces adjusted matching rate to original matching calculation, while setting $\mu = 1$ leads to the normalized matching rate. As μ grows, it is more probable to choose precise discriminators over generic, all-encompassing ones.

$$\text{matching}^*_\mu(k, \vec{x}) = \frac{\text{matching}(k, \vec{x})}{(|\Delta_k|)^{\mu/\delta}}. \tag{5}$$

5. Use Case: Clustering

In order to assess the applicability of the ideas just described, it is reported next the outcome of their use in various clustering tasks. Since WiSARD is a classifier, first of all its adaptation to unsupervised learning is described. The resulting method was named WiSARD for Clustering Data Streams, WCDS. Next, the performance of the WiSARD-based system when clustering 2D toy data sets is presented, as a proof of concept. At last, it is detailed WCDS use to cluster streaming observations from two large data sets.

WCDS architecture is similar to that of the original WiSARD, with one discriminator for each modeled pattern and RAM nodes as basic learning units. However, WCDS needs to identify unprecedented patterns during stream processing to create the respective discriminators. WiSARD does not require this because it learns based on training data ground truth, which is not available for clustering. In order to solve this matter, the following policy was established:

(1) for each streaming observation $\vec{x}$, the best matching discriminator Δ_k, $k = \mathrm{argmax}_k \ \mathrm{matching}^*_\mu(k, \vec{x})$, is identified;
(2) if $\mathrm{matching}^*_\mu(k, \vec{x}) < \epsilon$ (variable ϵ represents any tiny value, as 10^{-100}), a new discriminator is created to represent the novel pattern denoted by $\vec{x}$;
(3) otherwise, the best matching discriminator Δ_k records $\vec{x}$.

Another important feature of WCDS is its two-phase functioning.[18] That is, instead of trying to define the clusters directly from streaming data, the online maintenance of a collection of micro-clusters is used as an intermediate step of this process. These micro-clusters are updated during data stream processing, and feed an offline clustering procedure to generate high-level clusters. During WCDS offline functioning, the discriminators were aggregated according to a batch average-linkage agglomerative clustering algorithm. In this regard, Expression (6) was used to evaluate discriminators similarity.

$$s(\Delta_a, \Delta_b) = \frac{1 + \sum_i |\Delta_{a,i} \cap \Delta_{b,i}|}{1 + \sum_i |\Delta_{a,i} \cup \Delta_{b,i}|} \quad . \tag{6}$$

In the first set of experiments, WCDS obtained the clusters feeding from synthetic, bidimensional data sets, whose number of observations are in the range from over three hundreds to just over three thousands. No temporal information was considered during data processing. The five data sets used in this first set of experiments come from two publicly available data sets repositories: Jain, a 'two-moons'-like data set, and Aggregation, with 7 clusters in varied shapes, come from a collection found in the Web;[d] Complex8 and Complex9, which feature, respectively, 8 and 9 clusters in varied shapes can also be found in the Internet.[e] Such variety of characteristics poses an interesting test of learning adaptability.

The results of this first task are depicted in Fig. 2. WCDS was tested using the following parameter setup: $\delta = 200$ and unary encoding with $\gamma = 200$; since no aging was considered, $\omega = \infty$ and $\mu = 0$; the β parameter was adjusted to each data set, and its value is indicated together with the obtained results. The targeted number of clusters was considered to be known a priori. As shown, the clusters in all four tested scenarios were successfully determined. The worst result regarded the Complex8 data set, but they still led to a performance level over 0.9 with respect to the V-measure clustering validation index.[19]

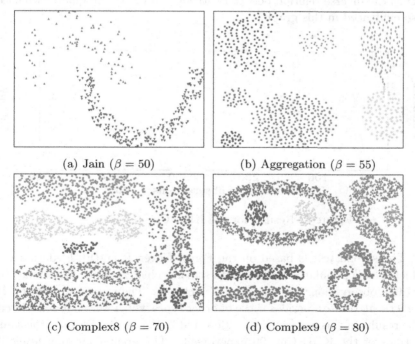

(a) Jain ($\beta = 50$) (b) Aggregation ($\beta = 55$)

(c) Complex8 ($\beta = 70$) (d) Complex9 ($\beta = 80$)

Figure 2: Clusters defined by WCDS for 2D toy data sets.

---

[d]http://cs.joensuu.fi/sipu/datasets/
[e]https://github.com/deric/clustering-benchmark

D.O. Cardoso, J. Gama & F. França

In the just described experiments, input data was processed as a single batch, targeting the definition of clusters just once. Alternatively, the observations can be considered as a stream of items, which can be used to establish current clusters according to data temporality. The next two experiments explore scenarios featuring streaming data. Both are based on regular data sets, whose elements are processed gradually. Current clusters were defined and evaluated every 1000 observations. This allowed to verify system sensitivity and responsiveness to concept drift.

This first test with data streams uses the KDD Cup 99 data set.[f] It is composed of 494,021 observations divided in 23 classes, which were processed in their original order. WCDS used the following setup: $\beta = 70, \delta = 50, \gamma = 50, \mu = 1$ and $\omega = 1000$. Figure 3 presents the results of the experiment with this data set. Observing the entropy plot, it can be noticed that during the intermediate section of the data stream there is a single class, what explains the null entropy in such period. Another interesting fact is the inverse relation between entropy and clustering quality which is also evidenced in this graph.

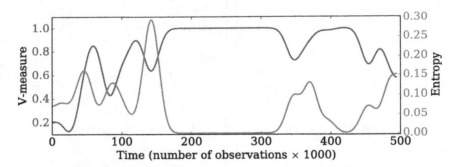

Figure 3: Results for the KDD Cup 99 data set.

The second test is based on the Forest Cover Type (FCT) data set,[20] which is also popularly used for data streams clustering benchmarking. Its 581,012 observations are elements of 7 classes. They are described by 10 numeric attributes, besides those of other types which were not considered. The results of this experiment are depicted in Fig. 4. WCDS used the same settings of the KDD Cup 99 experiment. The greater entropy levels of the FCT data set compared to those of the KDD Cup 99 data set are an

---

[f]http://kdd.ics.uci.edu/databases/kddcup99/

evidence of the bigger challenge the first represents compared to the last one. The small fluctuations of the V-measure values can be related to such higher entropy.

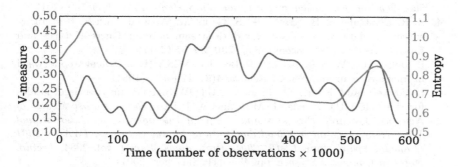

Figure 4: Results for the Forest Cover Type data set.

6. Conclusion

Learning from data streams is a research subject of major relevance nowadays. Accomplishing such goal is quite challenging, since it requires not only gathering meaningful information for the definition of high-level knowledge, but also meeting some efficiency targeting real-time processing of large volumes of streaming data. WiSARD can be seen as a valuable tool in this regard: it is flexible enough power applications in numerous scenarios, while having its low algorithmic complexity as one of its most patent features. This chapter provided some general guidelines for the adaptation of this model to feed from streaming data. Although some of its features can be used in this new context with no modification, it was shown that at least two aspects require careful reconsideration. The chapter discusses each of these aspects, providing some novel insights about the operation of this model which can be further developed. The subject addressed here is far from being exhausted: there is still much more to explore regarding data streams and the WiSARD model.

References

1. A. Bifet and R. Gavaldà. Learning from time-changing data with adaptive windowing. In *Proceedings of the Seventh SIAM International Conference on Data Mining, April 26-28, 2007, Minneapolis, Minnesota, USA*, pp. 443–448, SIAM (2007).

2. J. Gama, *Knowledge Discovery from Data Streams.* Chapman and Hall / CRC Data Mining and Knowledge Discovery Series, CRC Press (2010). ISBN 978-1-4398-2611-9.

3. H. Nguyen, Y. Woon, and W. K. Ng, A survey on data stream clustering and classification, *Knowledge and Information Systems* **45**(3), 535–569 (2015).

4. S. R. irez-Gallego, B. Krawczyk, S. G. ia, M. Wozniak, and F. Herrera, A survey on data preprocessing for data stream mining: Current status and future directions, *Neurocomputing.* **239**, 39–57 (2017).

5. I. Aleksander, W. Thomas, and P. Bowden, WiSARD, a radical step forward in image recognition, *Sensor Review.* **4**(3), 120–124 (1984).

6. I. Wickert and F. M. G. França. AUTOWISARD: unsupervised modes for the WISARD. In eds. J. Mira and A. Prieto, *Connectionist Models of Neurons, Learning Processes and Artificial Intelligence, 6th International Work-Conference on Artificial and Natural Neural Networks, IWANN 2001 Granada, Spain, June 13-15, 2001, Proceedings, Part I,* vol. 2084, *Lecture Notes in Computer Science,* pp. 435–441, Springer (2001).

7. D. O. Cardoso, F. M. G. França, and J. Gama. Clustering data streams using a forgetful neural model. In ed. S. Ossowski, *Proceedings of the 31st Annual ACM Symposium on Applied Computing, Pisa, Italy, April 4-8, 2016,* pp. 949–951, ACM (2016).

8. P. Coutinho, H. C. C. Carneiro, D. S. Carvalho, and F. M. G. França. Extracting rules from drasiw's "mental images". In *22th European Symposium on Artificial Neural Networks, ESANN 2014, Bruges, Belgium, April 23-25, 2014* (2014).

9. B. P. A. Grieco, P. M. V. Lima, M. D. Gregorio, and F. M. G. França, Producing pattern examples from "mental" images, *Neurocomputing.* **73**(7-9), 1057–1064 (2010).

10. D. S. de Carvalho, F. M. G. França, and P. M. V. Lima. Extracting semantic information from patent claims using phrasal structure annotations. In *2014 Brazilian Conference on Intelligent Systems, BRACIS 2014, Sao Paulo, Brazil, October 18-22, 2014,* pp. 31–36, IEEE Computer Society (2014).

11. H. C. C. Carneiro, F. M. G. França, and P. M. V. Lima, Multilingual part-of-speech tagging with weightless neural networks, *Neural Networks.* **66**, 11–21 (2015).

12. W. S. McCulloch and W. Pitts, A logical calculus of the ideas immanent in nervous activity, *The Bulletin of Mathematical Biophysics.* **5**(4), 115–133 (1943).

13. I. Aleksander, M. D. Gregorio, F. M. G. França, P. M. V. Lima, and H. Morton. A brief introduction to weightless neural systems. In *ESANN 2009, 17th European Symposium on Artificial Neural Networks, Bruges, Belgium, April 22-24, 2009, Proceedings* (2009).

14. A. Kolcz and N. Allinson, Application of the cmac input encoding scheme in the n-tuple approximation network, *Computers and Digital Techniques, IEE Proceedings* - **141**(3), 177–183 (May, 1994).

15. C. Linneberg and T. Jorgensen. Discretization methods for encoding of continuous input variables for boolean neural networks. In *Neural Networks,*

1999. IJCNN '99. International Joint Conference on, vol. 2, pp. 1219–1224 (Jul, 1999).

16. M. Datar and R. Motwani. The sliding-window computation model and results. In eds. M. N. Garofalakis, J. Gehrke, and R. Rastogi, *Data Stream Management - Processing High-Speed Data Streams*, Data-Centric Systems and Applications, pp. 149–165. Springer (2016).

17. D. O. Cardoso, M. D. Gregorio, P. M. V. Lima, J. Gama, and F. M. G. França. A weightless neural network-based approach for stream data clustering. In *Intelligent Data Engineering and Automated Learning - IDEAL 2012 - 13th International Conference, Natal, Brazil, August 29-31, 2012. Proceedings*, pp. 328–335, Springer (2012).

18. J. A. Silva, E. R. Faria, R. C. Barros, E. R. Hruschka, A. C. P. L. F. d. Carvalho, and J. a. Gama, Data stream clustering: A survey, *ACM Computing Surveys* **46**(1), 13:1–13:31 (July, 2013). ISSN 0360-0300.

19. A. Rosenberg and J. Hirschberg. V-measure: A conditional entropy-based external cluster evaluation measure. In ed. J. Eisner, *EMNLP-CoNLL 2007, Proceedings of the 2007 Joint Conference on Empirical Methods in Natural Language Processing and Computational Natural Language Learning, June 28-30, 2007, Prague, Czech Republic*, pp. 410–420, ACL (2007).

20. J. A. Blackard and D. J. Dean, Comparative accuracies of artificial neural networks and discriminant analysis in predicting forest cover types from cartographic variables, *Computers and Electronics in Agriculture*. **24**(3), 131–151 (1999).

Chapter 3

Ensemble Classifiers for Imbalanced and Evolving Data Streams

Dariusz Brzezinski* and Jerzy Stefanowski†

*Institute of Computing Science
Poznan University of Technology
Piotrowo 2, 60-965 Poznan*
*dbrzezinski@cs.put.poznan.pl
†jstefanowski@cs.put.poznan.pl

Stream classification is a challenging research field in which algorithms are required to process data online, use minimal resources, and react to concept changes. The task of mining incoming instances becomes even more demanding when the classifier is required to cope with imbalanced data — situations when one of the target classes is represented by much less instances than other classes. This chapter gives an overview of research on imbalanced stream classification. We present dedicated ensemble algorithms designed to cope with concept changes, discuss challenges posed by imbalanced class distributions along with assorted difficulty factors, and give an outlook on how class imbalance and concept changes can interact.

1. Introduction

Supervised classification is one of the most widely studied tasks in machine learning, data mining, statistics, and pattern recognition. Given a set of labeled training data, the task is to learn a relationship between values of attributes describing examples and a target class label.[1] This discovered relationship can then be used as a classifier to assign class values to unlabeled instances.

Numerous approaches to classification have already been proposed.[1,2] Out of these proposals, *ensembles* of classifiers have been proven to be particularly efficient at increasing predictive accuracy and decomposing more complex problems into easier sub-problems. An ensemble, also called a multiple classifier, is a set of individual component classifiers whose predictions are combined to assign a class label to a new instance. A good combination of classifiers requires that they are diversified, and many approaches to fulfill this criterion have been introduced.[3]

Most classification algorithms have been proposed for batch learning from static datasets that can be processed multiple times. However, the development of information technology and new applications have led to processing huge volumes of more complex data. In many domains, such as sensor networks, financial data prediction, mobile device tracking or network monitoring, data items arrive continuously in the form of *data streams*.

Compared to mining static data, the task of learning from data streams introduces unprecedented challenges, especially with respect to computational resources, as well as restrictions on making predictions in short time. Besides new processing requirements, another important challenge is that algorithms learning from streams often act in dynamic non-stationary environments, where the data and target concepts change over time in a phenomenon called *concept drift*.[4] Examples of real-life concept drifts include spam categorization, weather predictions, monitoring systems, financial fraud detection, and evolving customer preferences.[5]

As standard algorithms for supervised classification are not capable of meeting challenges presented by evolving data streams, several new algorithms have been proposed.[6,7] Out of a myriad of proposals, ensemble methods play an important role in reacting to many types of concept drift. Due to their modular architecture they are flexible to incorporate new data by either introducing a new component into the ensemble or updating knowledge of existing components. Moreover, voting weights of component classifiers can be tuned with respect to recent data elements.[8]

Many practical applications make learning classifiers from streams even more challenging by introducing additional data complexities. One of such additional challenges is *class imbalance*, i.e., a situation when one of the target classes is highly underrepresented. Class imbalance is an obstacle even for learning from static data, as standard learning algorithms are usually biased toward better recognition of the majority classes and have difficulties in correctly classifying new objects from the minority class. Since several years, the class imbalance problem has been studied in this static data framework and many new algorithms have already been introduced; for their comprehensive review see recent monographs and surveys.[9–11]

However, the classification of imbalanced data is a relatively new research topic in the stream mining community. An evolving and imbalanced stream is a more demanding classification framework than a static dataset.

Due to the evolving nature of data streams, it is possible that the imbalance ratio and the notion of a minority class may change over time. A more complex scenario will occur when these changes are accompanied by concept drifts such as moving decision boundaries or other changes in class example distributions. Making predictions becomes even more ambitious when multiple minority classes occur in the stream and novel classes may appear.[12] Additionally, class imbalance introduces challenges to classifier performance measures and evaluation procedures used in stream mining.[13,14]

This chapter describes recent advances that have been made in the field of imbalanced data streams classification. In our opinion, it is still an open research task which requires novel studies and whose analysis may lead to many interesting results. Besides presenting current state-of-the-art in ensemble algorithms for imbalanced streams, we would like to draw the reader's attention to the limitations of existing approaches and position new research directions.

The remainder of the chapter is organized as follows. Section 2 gives a more formal presentation of data stream classification and discusses basic approaches to coping with concept drift. In Section 3, we describe the class imbalance problem and other data difficulty factors connected with imbalanced class distributions. Section 4 reviews the state-of-the-art in imbalanced stream classifiers, whereas Section 5 showcases potential interactions between class imbalance and concept drift. Finally, Section 6 concludes the chapter with an outlook on potential future research directions in the field.

2. Data Streams

Before analyzing challenges posed by imbalanced streams, let us explain the basic concepts and definitions concerning data stream classification.

A data stream can be defined as a sequence of labeled examples $\{\mathbf{x}^t, y^t\}$ for $t = 1, 2, \ldots, T$, where $\mathbf{x}$ is a vector of attribute values and y is a class label ($y \in \{K_1, \ldots, K_l\}$).[15] When a new example $\mathbf{x}^t$ arrives it is classified by a classifier, which predicts its class label. Most studies[6,7] consider a completely supervised framework where after some time the true class label y^t is available and can be used to update the classifier.[a]

Since data streams can be potentially unbounded, the entire sequence of examples cannot not be made available to a classifier at once. Moreover,

---

[a]We note that there are several works concerning active learning and delayed labeling in stream mining, however, as they do not concern imbalanced data, we focus solely on the completely supervised framework.

it is usually assumed that the time required to process a single instance and the average memory usage should remain constant throughout the life of a stream classifier.[6] This forces data stream algorithms to process data in smaller fragments, either *online* or in *blocks* (also called *data chunks*). In the first approach, algorithms process single examples appearing one by one in consecutive moments in time, while in the other approach, examples are available only in larger sets called data blocks $B_1, B_2, \ldots, B_j$. Blocks are usually of equal size and the construction, evaluation, or update of classifiers is done when all examples from a new block are available.

The distinction between online and block processing also refers to classifier evaluation procedures. Contrary to batch learning scenarios, it is assumed that due to the size and speed of data streams repeated runs over the data are not necessary to estimate classifier performance on labeled testing examples. Furthermore, due to their computational costs, re-sampling techniques such as cross-validation or bootstrapping are deemed too expensive for streams.[15] As a result, simpler error-estimation procedures are used, yet ones that build a picture of performance over time, either after each example or consecutive blocks. The most popular of such procedures involves interleaving testing with training. In practice, this means that each individual example (or block of examples) is first used to test the classifier before it is used for training.[16] If concept drifts are expected, this scheme is usually modified to calculate evaluation measures using only the most recent data, rather than the entire stream. Such incremental assessment with forgetting is often denoted as *prequential evaluation*.

As it was mentioned in the introduction, alongside restrictions concerning processing time and memory usage data streams are characterized by their potential to change over time, a phenomenon that is often referred to as *concept drift*.[4] More formally, if in each point in time t, every example is generated by a source with a joint distribution $P^t(\mathbf{x}, y)$ over the data and all examples are generated by the same distribution, we say that concepts in data are *stable*. However, if for two distinct points in time t and $t + \Delta$ an $\mathbf{x}$ exists such that $P^t(\mathbf{x}, y) \neq P^{t+\Delta}(\mathbf{x}, y)$, then concept drift occurs.[6] Although different component probabilities of $P^t(\mathbf{x}, y)$ may change,[4] in case of supervised classification most studies are mainly interested in *real drift*, that is changes in posterior probabilities of classes $P(y|\mathbf{x})$. Nevertheless, it is worth noticing that changes of imbalance ratios over time are also changes in class distributions $P(y)$ and, therefore, can be considered a special case of *virtual drift*. Concept drifts introduce further difficulties to data stream processing and force classifiers to forget outdated examples and adapt to new concepts. The task of actively recognizing and reacting to drifts is particularly challenging, as changes can occur suddenly, gradually, or reoccur after some time.[17]

The aforementioned challenges inspired a range of novel classifiers designed specifically to cope with evolving streams of data. These classifiers can be divided into *active* (trigger-based) approaches, which introduce changes in classifiers when drifts are detected, and *passive* (adaptive) approaches, which continuously update the classifier regardless of whether drifts occur in the data stream or not.[4]

Trigger-based approaches include drift detectors that analyze incoming examples and indicate the need for rebuilding a classifier. Drift detectors are usually implemented using statistical tests based on sequential analysis, process control charts, or monitoring differences between two distributions.[4] Detectors based on sequential analysis check whether the classification error calculated on the most recent instances is significantly different from its value calculated on a range of older instances. In drift detectors based on control charts each classifier prediction is treated as a Bernoulli trail. Then, the number of classification errors can be modeled with a binomial distribution, which in turn can be tested for significantly improbable changes.[18] Finally, several approaches use a reference window which is compared with a sliding window of the most recent examples. If the distributions over these two windows are significantly different, a change is signaled, suggesting that only examples from the sliding window should be used to create a new model.[19]

Adaptive methods operate in a different manner — they try to update the classifier without explicit change detection. One general approach to adapt classifiers to evolving streams includes using a *sliding window*, which moves over processed examples and ensures that only the most recent data is used to train a classifier. Some techniques use windows of a fixed size, however, this introduces the problem of choosing a proper size for a given stream (larger window sizes are more useful for slower concept drifts, but fail whenever sudden drifts occur). Alternatively, dynamic adjusting of the window size can also be applied.[20–22] Apart from windowing approaches, several innately incremental classifiers have been proposed. Probably the most representative of such classifiers is the Very Fast Decision Tree (VFDT or Hoeffding Tree)[23] algorithm, which induces a decision tree from a data stream incrementally, without the need for storing examples after they have been used to update the tree. Hoeffding Trees work similarly to classic tree induction algorithms and differ mainly in the selection of the split attribute, which is done without viewing all the examples but guarantees the right split with a user-specified probability. Although the original VFDT algorithm did not take into account concept drifts, currently there exist several modifications of the algorithm that involve a forgetting mechanism.[6]

However, the majority of studies on time-changing data streams involve the use of *ensemble classifiers*. Due to their modular construction, ensembles are capable of adapting to changing streams by introducing new components created using batches of incoming examples, updating existing component classifiers, or changing weights in the aggregation phase. Depending on the way component classifiers are created and updated, data stream ensembles are categorized into block-based and online approaches.

Block-based ensembles re-evaluate components with fixed-size blocks of incoming instances and usually replace the worst component with a new candidate classifier trained on the most recent examples. The first of such block-based ensembles was the Streaming Ensemble Algorithm (SEA),[24] which used a heuristic replacement strategy based on accuracy and diversity. Using these two factors, after each block of examples SEA reevaluates a set of decision trees and substitutes the weakest classifier with a new decision tree trained on examples from the most recent block. Following a similar scheme, many other bock-based ensembles were put forward, e.g. the Accuracy Weighted Ensemble,[25] Learn^{++}NSE,[26] or the Accuracy Updated Ensemble.[17]

Referring to online ensembles, one of the first proposed algorithms was the Weighted Majority Algorithm,[27] which combines the predictions of a set of component classifiers and updates their weights when they make false predictions. Another popular online ensemble is Online Bagging,[28] a generalization of batch bagging known from static environments, proposed by Oza and Russell. It uses incremental learners as component classifiers and mimics bootstrap sampling by using single examples multiple times according to the Poisson distribution. Other reference online ensembles include: the DDD algorithm,[29] Dynamic Weighted Majority (DWM),[30] or the Online Accuracy Updated Ensemble.[31] A broader categorization and discussion on ensemble classifiers for evolving data streams can be found in recent surveys.[7,32,33]

The aforementioned concepts and algorithms focus on three main challenges posed by data stream classification: limited time, memory restrictions, and concept changes. In the following section, we discuss other difficulty factors that can make classification problems even more challenging.

3. Class Imbalance and Data Difficulty Factors

The class imbalance problem typically concerns binary classification or binarized multi-class problems, where one class (called a *minority class*) is under-represented in comparison to the remaining classes (*majority class*). Correct recognition of the minority class is of key importance and misclassification of minority examples is more severe than incorrectly predicting the majority class. We recall that standard classification algorithms tend to focus on majority classes and, therefore, give unsatisfactory results in imbalanced domains.[9]

It is worth noting that imbalanced data constitute a challenge not only when constructing a classifier, but also when evaluating its performance. Indeed, an overall classification accuracy is not the best criterion characterizing performance of a classifier as it is biased toward recognizing examples from the majority classes. Since good recognition of minority examples is preferred, measures other than classification accuracy were defined on the basis of the confusion matrix. To strike a balance between majority and minority class performance, many researchers consider sensitivity and specificity. Sensitivity (also called recall) is the ratio of correctly recognized examples from the minority class, whereas specificity is the ratio of examples correctly excluded from the majority classes. Kubat and Matwin[34] proposed to aggregate these measures through a geometric mean (G-mean). A popular alternative, called the F-measure, involves aggregating precision and recall using the harmonic mean. Furthermore, in case of scoring classifiers the area under the Receiver Operator Characteristic curve (AUC) is typically exploited; Japkowicz and Shah[35] present a comprehensive review of these and other measures dedicated for evaluating classifiers on imbalance data.

Recent studies show that the problem of class imbalance is usually accompanied by additional difficulty factors. In some problems characterized by high imbalance, standard classifiers were found sufficiently accurate,[36] whereas series of experimental evaluations have proven that, when there is a clear separation between classes, the minority class can be sufficiently recognized regardless of the high imbalance ratio.[37] These and other studies have led to conclusions that the *global class imbalance ratio*[b] is not necessarily the only, or even the main, problem causing the degradation

---

[b]Global imbalance ratio is usually expressed as either $N^{min}:N^{maj}$ or N^{min}/N, where N^{maj}, N^{min}, N are the number of majority, minority, and total of examples in the dataset, respectively.

of classification performance. Therefore, focusing only on the global ratio may be insufficient for improving classification performance.[38–42] Following these opinions, in this chapter we draw our attention to other characteristics of instance distributions in the attribute space. These characteristics are often called *data complexity* or *data difficulty factors*. Although these data factors should affect learning also in balanced domains, when they occur *together* with class imbalance the deterioration of classification performance is amplified and affects mostly (or sometimes only) the minority class. Researchers usually distinguish the following data difficulty factors: decomposing the minority class into rare sub-concepts, overlapping between classes, and presence of outliers, rare instances, or noise. Examples of these complexity factors are illustrated in Fig. 1.

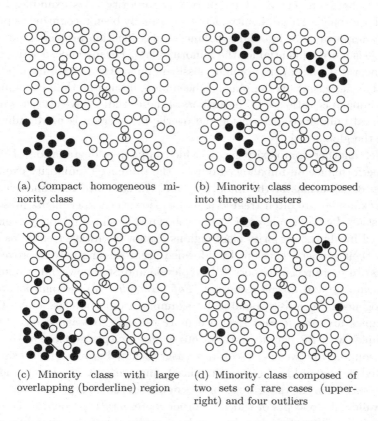

(a) Compact homogeneous minority class

(b) Minority class decomposed into three subclusters

(c) Minority class with large overlapping (borderline) region

(d) Minority class composed of two sets of rare cases (upper-right) and four outliers

Fig. 1. Examples of minority class distributions with different difficulty factors. Minority examples are depicted as black circles, majority examples as white circles.

The influence of *class decomposition* has been noticed by Japkowicz *et al.*[38,43] Their experimental studies with mainly artificial datasets have clearly demonstrated that the degradation of classification performance has resulted from the decomposition of the minority class into many sub-parts containing very few examples, rather than from changing the global imbalance ratio. They have also argued that the minority class often does not form a compact homogeneous distribution of the single concept, but is scattered into many smaller sub-clusters surrounded by majority examples. Such sub-clusters of minority examples often play the role of *small disjuncts*,[43] which are harder to learn and cause more classification errors than larger sub-concepts.

Other factors related to the class distribution are linked to high *overlapping* between regions of minority and majority class examples in the attribute space. This difficulty factor has already been recognized as particularly important for standard, balanced, classification problems, however, its role is more influential for the minority class. For instance, a series of experimental studies of six popular classifiers on synthetic data have pointed out that increasing overlapping has been more influential than changing the class imbalance ratio.[39,44] The authors of these studies have also shown that the local imbalance ratio inside the overlapping region is more influential than the global ratio.

Yet another complexity factor which influences degradation of classifier performance on imbalanced data is the presence of minority examples inside distributions of the majority class. In standard machine learning, such examples are often treated as noise. However, experiments presented in a study by Napierala *et al.*[45] have shown that single minority examples located inside the majority class regions cannot be always treated as noise since their proper treatment by informed preprocessing may improve classifiers. In more recent papers[40,41] Napierala and Stefanowski distinguished between safe and unsafe examples. *Safe examples* are the ones located in homogeneous regions populated by examples from one class only. Other examples are *unsafe* and they are more difficult to learn from. Unsafe examples were further categorized into *borderline* (placed close to the decision boundary between classes), *rare cases* (isolated groups of few examples located deeper inside the opposite class), and *outliers*. Napierala and Stefanowski also argue that rare examples or outliers could represent very small but valid sub-concepts of which no other representatives could be collected for training. Therefore, they cannot be considered as noisy examples which typically would be removed or re-labeled. The same authors introduced an approach[40,41] to automatically identify the aforementioned types of examples in real world data sets by analyzing class labels of examples in the local neighborhood of a considered example. Finally, other studies[42] emphasize that several of the aforementioned data factors usually occur together in real world imbalanced data sets.

Various methods to handle class imbalance have already been proposed.[9–11] In general, they are categorized into *data level* and *algorithm level* approaches.

Methods within the first category are classifier-independent. They are applied in a preprocessing step and attempt to modify the class distribution inside the training data toward a more balanced one.[11] The simplest data preprocessing techniques are *random over-sampling*, which replicates examples from the minority class, and *random under-sampling*, which randomly eliminates examples from the majority classes until a required degree of balance between classes is reached. However, the simplest re-balancing may not be sufficient to improve learning classifiers. The focused (also called *informed*) methods, which consider internal characteristics of regions around minority class examples, are often exploited, see e.g. SMOTE [46] and its extensions, one-side-sampling, NCR, or SPIDER.[45] The most popular among the informed methods is SMOTE, which considers each example from the minority class and generates new synthetic examples along the lines between the selected example and some of its randomly selected k-nearest neighbors from the minority class. A comprehensive review of re-sampling methods for imbalanced data can be found in a survey by Branco *et al.*[10]

The second category, algorithm level methods, involves specific solutions dedicated to improving a given classifier. They usually include modifications of the learning algorithm, its classification strategy, or adaptation to the cost sensitive framework. Within the algorithm level approaches, ensembles are also quite often applied. These new proposed solutions usually either employ preprocessing methods before learning component classifiers or embed the cost-sensitive framework in the ensemble learning process.[47,48] Most of these ensembles are based on known strategies from bagging, boosting, random forests, or their variants to cost learning.

For instance, the most efficient generalizations of bagging apply random or informed preprocessing to change balance between classed in bootstrap samples. *Under-bagging* approaches randomly reduce the number of the majority class examples in each bootstrap sample to the cardinality of the minority class. The best performing Roughly Balanced Bagging approximates these numbers from the negative binomial distribution.[49,50] On the other hand, in *over-bagging* the minority examples are additionally resampled to bootstraps.[51]

4. Classifiers for Imbalanced Streams

The number of classifiers which address imbalanced and evolving data streams is fairly limited. Most of them are adaptations of ensembles for evolving streams extended by simple re-sampling mechanisms known from static data mining, like under-bagging or over-bagging. Moreover, the employed re-sampling techniques are parametrized based on the global imbalanced ratio. In general, ensembles for imbalanced streams could be categorized in three ways, based on:

- processing streams in data blocks or online;
- using under-sampling or over-sampling;
- adaptive or drift-detector-based classifiers.

One of the first proposals by Gao *et al.*[52] divides the stream into blocks $B_1, B_2, \ldots, B_j$. Each block B_j contains N_j^{min} minority class examples and N_j^{maj} majority examples. N_j^{min} is assumed to be much smaller than N_j^{maj}. The main idea while building a new classifier from a given block is to take all minority examples from the previous blocks ($B_k, k < j$) and undersample the majority examples from the current block (with respect to a given global imbalance ratio). Such sampling gives a new temporary subset T_s. Subsequently, m datasets are generated from T_s in the following way: each majority example is randomly propagated into exactly one of m sets (completely disjoint) while minority examples are propagated to all of these m sets. From each of the m sets a component classifier is built and added to the ensemble, where predictions of these components are combined using simple voting. In general, this idea resembles the simplest under-bagging solutions known from static batch data.[50,51]

To accommodate a potentially infinite data stream, Gao *et al.* propose to sample minority examples from only a limited number of the most recent blocks, using either fixed (each block contributes equally) or fading (the more recent blocks contribute more instances) strategy. However, as all of the minority examples are used to learn each classifier, this method is limited to situations with a stable definition of the minority class.

Based on a critical discussion of the proposal of Gao *et al.*, Chen and He proposed the Selectively Recursive Approach (SERA).[53] Instead of using all minority class examples, SERA selectively looks for a limited number of the most similar examples to instances of the minority class inside the current block. The best n examples are found based on the Mahalanobis distance and combined with all majority class examples in a given block. After selecting the most relevant examples the authors propose to construct either a single new classifier or a bagging ensemble (this has also led to a slightly different variant in Multiple Selectively Recursive Approach[54]). Unlike the proposal of Gao *et al.*, SERA can be considered an over-sampling approach.

In their further work, Chen and He extend the idea of sampling examples from previous blocks to the Recursive Ensemble Approach (REA).[55] The first novelty in REA is balancing the current block by adding those minority instances from previous blocks which are nearest neighbors of the minority examples in the current training block. Following the authors' motivations, this approach should perform better than previous proposals when the minority class is decomposed into smaller sub-concepts. Another extension involves using a non-linear weighting function for each component classifier in the ensemble's voting aggregation. These functions are based on mean square errors calculated on the the new block of testing examples. According to experimental results, REA and SERA provide more accurate predictions than the proposal of Gao *et al.*[53,55]

Lichtenwalter and Chawla proposed another extension of the work by Gao *et al.*, where instead of propagating all minority class examples, they also propagate misclassified majority class instances.[56] With this approach, the authors seek to better define the boundary between the classes, thereby, increasing the performance of ensemble members. Their other novel contribution is the adaption of the Hellinger distance (a skew-insensitive metric) to measure similarities between two data blocks and, thus, to implicitly check if a concept drift has taken place. This information is then used to weight ensemble members during the aggregation of their predictions with a linear block-dissimilarity weighting function.

Another use of Hellinger distances was presented by Hoens and Chawla.[57] First they criticize the simple temporal similarity commonly used to propagate examples, and promote the selection of old instances that are drawn from the most similar distribution as the new minority class examples. They solve this task by reclassifying old blocks with a variant of the Naive Bayes classifier constructed from the recent blocks. Then, they provide a modification to the Heuristic Updatable Weighted Random Subspaces algorithm (HUWRS), where each component classifier is built on a different set of features and combined with the aforementioned idea of using Hellinger distances.

Furthermore, Ditzler and Polikar[58] considered extending their Learn^{++}.NSE algorithm for the case of class imbalance. This combines their previous approach to learning in non-stationary scenarios with the idea of bagging, where under-sampling is performed in each bag. Component classifiers are weighted based on their performance on both minority and majority classes, thus, preventing significant loss of accuracy on majority examples. However, one must point out that this approach assumes a well-defined minority class and cannot handle dynamically changing properties of classes. These authors also studied a different variant which employs oversampling of the minority class.

Another idea of selective sampling in block-based ensembles was considered by Zhang *et al.*[59] They propose to use the k-means algorithm to form clusters of majority examples in the current training block and then calculate their centroids. The number of these clusters is set to be equal to the number of minority examples in the current block. Then, a current training set is constructed by taking all minority examples along with centroids of the clusters and used to build a new classifier which is added to an ensemble. The current component classifiers are evaluated on the recent block with the AUC measure and these results are used for estimating the weight of components and selecting best classifiers to be included in the ensemble. The same authors proposed another approach called ECSDS (Ensemble Classifier for Skewed Data Streams), which additionally aims at reducing the learning time by limiting the number ensemble updates.

A much smaller body of work is dedicated to learning ensembles online, instance by instance. One of the main motivations for online solutions for imbalanced data follows observations that these algorithms may react to drifts faster than block-based classifiers, where the update is delayed to the end of the block. The simplest idea of updating component classifiers online depending of the imbalance ratio was discussed by Nguyen *et al.*[60]

More advanced online approaches to imbalanced and drifting streams were proposed by Wang *et al.*[61,62] Unlike previously discussed papers, these authors considered variations of the imbalance ratio over time. Furthermore, they noticed that the role of classes may evolve, for example, the majority class may become the minority over time.

First, Wang *et al.*[61] proposed two basic extensions of online bagging — its oversampling and undersampling variants. In the first version when the incoming example belongs to the minority class, it increases the chance of adding its copies to component classifiers by changing the parameter of the Poisson distribution in online bagging. The value of this parameter is related to the imbalance ratio. In the same way the chance for selecting copies of the majority class is reduced in the undersampling based variant. To cope with dynamically changing imbalance ratios and potential switching of class roles, the authors propose a dedicated concept drift detector. Its output directly influences the parameter of the Poisson distribution in oversampling or undersampling. A further modification of this idea, called WEOB, used a combination of both under and oversampling in order to chose the better strategy for the current state of the stream. An adaptive weighting combination scheme was proposed to accommodate this hybrid solution, where weights of these sampling strategies are either computed as their G-mean values or are only one of them is selected. Recently, a multi-class extension of this method has also been proposed.[12]

Finally, two other, less typical, proposals concern ensembles of online neural networks to handle drifting and imbalanced streams. Ghazikhani *et al.*[63] embedded elements of cost-sensitive learning into the process of neural network training. Similarly, the Ensemble of Subset Online Sequential Extreme Learning Machine (ESOS-ELM) was developed by Mirza *et al.*,[64] where randomized neural networks were trained on balanced subsets of the stream. However, these proposals do not adapt to changes of the minority class like the aforementioned approaches of Wang *et al.*

5. Interactions Between Class Imbalance and Concept Drift

In this section, we will showcase possible interactions between class imbalance, concept drift, and additional difficulty factors in the form of minority class sub-clusters. For this purpose, we will analyze experimental evaluations of ensemble classifiers including one of the most popular ensembles for imbalanced streams — SERA.[53]

The presented analysis is based on an experimental setup from our recent study on evaluating stream classifiers using AUC calculated incrementally with forgetting.[14] Although the cited work focuses mainly on evaluation measures, parts of the results therein can be used to highlight difficulties posed by evolving data difficulty factors. The analysis of these results will serve as a vantage point for positioning lines of future research in the field of imbalanced stream classification.

5.1. *Experimental Setup*

We present experiments involving four classifiers:

- Very Fast Decision Tree (VFDT),[6]
- Online Bagging (Bag),[28]
- Accuracy Updated Ensemble (AUE),[17]
- Selectively Recursive Approach (SERA).[53]

The Very Fast Decision Tree (VFDT) was chosen as a reference classifier without any forgetting mechanism. The remaining three algorithms are ensemble classifiers representing: an online approach (Bag), a block-based approach with forgetting (AUE), and a dynamic block-based oversampling method designed for imbalanced streams (SERA).

All the algorithms and evaluation methods were implemented in Java as part of the MOA framework.[65] All ensemble methods (Bag, AUE, SERA) used 10 Very Fast Decision Trees as base learners, AUE and SERA were set to create new components every $d = 1000$ examples.

Classifiers were evaluated using six measures: accuracy, AUC, G-mean, Cohen's Kappa, Kappa M, and Recall. These measures can be defined using a two-class confusion matrix presented in Table 1.

Table 1.   Confusion matrix for two-class classification

Actual \ Predicted	Positive	Negative	total
Positive	TP	FN	P
Negative	FP	TN	N
total	$\hat{P}$	$\hat{N}$	n

The *TP* (*True Positive*) and *TN* (*True Negative*) entries denote the number of examples classified correctly by the classifier as minority and majority instances, while the *FN* (*False Negative*) and *FP* (*False Positive*) indicate the number of misclassified minority and majority examples, respectively. Based on these values, the evaluation measures used in the experiments are defined as follows:

$$\text{Accuracy} = \frac{TP + TN}{TP + TN + FP + FN}$$

$$\text{AUC} = \int_{\infty}^{-\infty} \text{TPR}(T)\text{FPR}'(T)\, dT = P(X_P > X_N)$$

$$\text{G-mean} = \sqrt{\frac{TP}{TP + FN} \cdot \frac{TN}{FP + TN}}$$

$$\text{Kappa} = \frac{p_0 - p_c}{1 - p_c}$$

$$\text{Kappa M} = \frac{p_0 - p_m}{1 - p_m}$$

$$\text{Recall} = \frac{TP}{TP + FN}$$

where X_P is the classifier score for a minority instance and X_N is the score for a majority instance, p_0 is the accuracy of the tested classifier, p_c is the accuracy of a chance classifier, and p_m is the accuracy of a classifier always predicting the majority class. A detailed description of each evaluation measure can be found, for example, in a recent publication by Japkowicz and Shah.[35] These measures where calculated prequentially,[16] i.e., incrementally with forgetting, using a sliding window of $d = 1000$ examples.

5.2. *Datasets*

A key component when assessing the impact of different difficulty factors is testing classifiers in a controlled environment. Therefore, for this study we use 11 synthetic datasets created using custom stream generators, which enabled us to administer the evolution of class imbalance, concepts, and minority sub-clusters. Additionally, we use two real-world data streams which showcase both class imbalance and changes over time.

The Ratio datasets are designed to test classifier performance under different imbalance ratios without drift. Examples from the minority class create a uniform five-dimensional sphere, whereas majority class examples are uniformly distributed outside that sphere. The Dis datasets are created in a similar manner, but the minority class is fragmented into spherical sub-clusters (playing the role of small disjuncts). Datasets Dis_2, Dis_3, Dis_5 have 2, 3, and 5 clusters, respectively. In the AppDis datasets, every stream begins with a single well-defined cluster, and additional clusters are added as the stream progresses. New disjuncts appear suddenly in majority class space after 40 k ($\text{AppDis}_{2,3,5}$), 50 k ($\text{AppDis}_{3,5}$), 60 k, and 70 k (AppDis_5) examples. In static data mining, the problem of small disjuncts is known to be more problematic than class imbalance per se,[38] however, to the best of our knowledge this issue has not been tackled in stream classification. Finally, datasets MinMaj, Gradual_{RC}, and Sudden_{RC} contain class ratio changes over time. In MinMaj, the majority class abruptly becomes the minority; such a virtual drift relates to a problem recently discussed by Wang *et al.*[62] Sudden$_{RC}$ was created using a modified version of the SEA generator,[24] and contains three sudden class ratio changes (1:1/1:100/1:10/1:1) appearing every 25 k examples. Analogously, Gradual$_{RC}$ uses a modified Hyperplane generator,[25] and simulates a continuous ratio change from 1:1 to 1:100 throughout the entire stream. Sudden$_{RC}$ has attributes with values ranging from 0 to 10, whereas all the remaining synthetic datasets have attribute values uniformly distributed in the range $[-1, 1]$. The two real world dataset used are KDDCup and PAKDD.[66,67] It is worth noting that we used the smaller version of the KDDCup dataset and transformed it into a binary classification problem, by combining every class other than "NORMAL" into one "ATTACK" class. The characteristics of all the datasets are given in Table 2.

Table 2.   Characteristic of datasets

Dataset	#Inst	#Attrs	Class ratio	Noise	#Drifts	Drift type
Ratio$_{5050}$	100 k	5	1:1	0%	0	none
Ratio$_{1090}$	100 k	5	1:9	0%	0	none
Ratio$_{0595}$	100 k	5	1:19	0%	0	none
Ratio$_{0199}$	100 k	5	1:99	0%	0	none
Dis$_2$	100 k	5	1:9	0%	0	none
Dis$_3$	100 k	5	1:9	0%	0	none
Dis$_5$	100 k	5	1:9	0%	0	none
AppDis$_2$	100 k	5	1:9	0%	1	sudden
AppDis$_3$	100 k	5	1:9	0%	2	sudden
AppDis$_5$	100 k	5	1:9	0%	4	sudden
MinMaj	100 k	5	1:19/19:1	0%	1	sud. virt.
Gradual$_{RC}$	100 k	3	1:1 → 1:100	5%	1	grad. virt.
Sudden$_{RC}$	100 k	3	1:1/1:100/1:10/1:1	10%	3	rec. virt.
KDDCup	494 k	41	~1:4	-	-	unknown
PAKDD	50 k	30	~1:4	-	-	unknown

5.3. *Results*

We experimentally compared classifier evaluations using accuracy, AUC, G-mean, Cohen's Kappa, Kappa M, and Recall.[14] Here we focus on the interactions between difficulty factors and their effect on different classifiers. To facilitate the presentation of results, we will mostly concentrate on plots depicting classifier performance using the G-mean measure; more detailed results are available in publications by Brzezinski and Stefanowski.[14] Figure 2 presents selected plots, which characterize different difficulty factors.

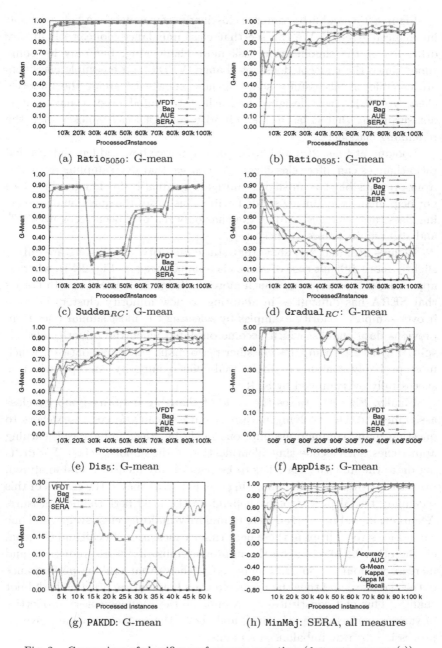

(a) Ratio$_{5050}$: G-mean

(b) Ratio$_{0595}$: G-mean

(c) Sudden$_{RC}$: G-mean

(d) Gradual$_{RC}$: G-mean

(e) Dis$_5$: G-mean

(f) AppDis$_5$: G-mean

(g) PAKDD: G-mean

(h) MinMaj: SERA, all measures

Fig. 2.   Comparison of classifier performance over time (**dataset**: measure(s)).

Figures 2(a) and 2(b) compare classifier performance on a balanced and imbalanced stream. We can see that class imbalance alone, without any drift, makes the classification task more challenging, but only for some time. Since the concept does not change, VFDT and ensemble classifiers are capable of successfully adapting new knowledge about the minority class. As SERA was designed for such static imbalanced scenarios, it is not surprising that it learns the minority concept much quicker than the remaining classifiers.

Looking at Figs. 2(c) and 2(d), one can notice how sudden and gradual ratio changes can affect classifiers. We can see that oversampling examples from previous blocks can slightly mitigate gradual ratio changes, but does not help in any way during sudden drift. This raises the question of detecting class ratio changes, a topic that has only recently been recognized[62,68] and still requires more studies.

Figures 2(e) and 2(f) show that static minority sub-clusters are only a slightly more difficult case of static class imbalance (see Fig. 2(b)), whereas appearing sub-concepts are much more challenging. It is also worth noting that SERA has difficulties in adapting to new minority clusters because it over-samples minority examples by selecting the most similar ones from previous data chunks, which become outdated when the minority class is split. Figure 2(g) compares classifier performance on a real dataset, which most probably contains a single, well-defined minority concept, which is successfully oversampled by SERA.

Finally, Fig. 2(h) raises the issue of changing majority-minority class assignments. The evolving nature of data streams forces researchers to question many common assumptions made by static imbalanced learning approaches, such as one-time identification of the minority class. For drifting data, the minority class has to be periodically identified and analyzed, prior to any over- or under-sampling. As Fig. 2(h) shows, the results of this seemingly trivial task strongly depend on the used performance measure. Accuracy, κ, and κ_m are sensitive to minority-majority class swaps, and one can notice strong drops in these performance measures. Recall and G-mean, on the other hand, focus on the improving minority class predictions and increase without dropping. Finally, AUC shows that ranking performance of the classifier, and thus the predicted class boundaries, practically did not change. This plot constitutes an example of the complementary properties of various performance measures, and shows the impact they can have on processing drifting imbalanced streams.

6. Outlook

The literature review and experimental analysis presented in this chapter show the vast number of research problems related to mining imbalanced and evolving data streams. Popular block-based and incremental ensembles can react to changes over time, but recognize minority class concepts much slower than specialized oversampling approaches such as SERA. However, over- or under-sampling methods alone are not capable of coping with the myriad of possible interactions between class imbalance and concept drift. Sudden class ratio changes or appearing minority sub-clusters require novel change reaction mechanisms, since current drift detectors are mostly designed for balanced data. As showcased in the experimental analysis, this in turn raises the broader question of using evaluation measures suited for imbalanced streams. Although some of these issues have recently started to gain attention,[14,62] solutions to these problems are still to be found.

Moreover, the intersection of class imbalance and data stream mining still holds many problems that have not been explored. Current research concentrates on binary classification, while recent studies[12] show that in multi-class problems one can expect concept drifts in the form of appearing novel minority classes. Moreover, the evolving nature of data streams has still not been studied in the context of data difficulty factors recently recognized in static classification of imbalanced data.[41] The same way as sub-clusters can suddenly appear they could also appear gradually, reoccur, or move within the attribute space. Class overlapping could also change over time, for example, the borderline region between two classes could grow, shrink, or change its shape. Notions of rare cases and outliers are another set of difficulty factors that still have not been properly introduced to data stream mining. All the mentioned complexities provide a fertile ground for research on adaptive systems.

We hope that this chapter will not only serve as reference for current state-of-the-art in classifiers for imbalanced and drifting data streams, but will also inspire new works in this field. New adaptive ensembles capable of dealing with various difficulty factors are still sought for. Similarly, evaluation measures and drift detectors tailored for various drifts in imbalanced streams are still to be studied. However, to make these advancements possible, potential types of drift between difficulty factors have to be recognized. We believe that these issues are of vital importance, because, as research in the field of class imbalance has shown, data complexities have a much more profound impact on classifier performance than class imbalance alone.

Acknowledgments

Results presented in this chapter were funded by the Polish National Science Center under Grant No. DEC-2013/11/B/ST6/00963. Dariusz Brzezinski acknowledges the support of an FNP START scholarship.

References

1. C. Aggarwal. An introduction to data classification. In ed. C. Aggarwal, *Data Classification: Algorithms and Applications*, pp. 1–36. Chapman and Hall (2015).
2. O. Maimon and L. Rokach, eds., *Data Mining and Knowledge Discovery Handbook*, second edn. Springer (2010).
3. L. I. Kuncheva, *Combining Pattern Classifiers: Methods and Algorithms*. Wiley-Interscience (2004).
4. J. Gama, I. Zliobaite, A. Bifet, M. Pechenizkiy, and A. Bouchachia, A survey on concept drift adaptation, *ACM Comput. Surv.* **46**(4), 44:1–44:37 (2014).
5. I. Zliobaite, M. Pechenizkiy, and J. Gama. An overview of concept drift applications. In eds. N. Japkowicz and J. Stefanowski, *Big Data Analysis: New Algorithms for a New Society*, vol. 16, *Studies in Big Data*, pp. 91–114. Springer (2016).
6. J. Gama, *Knowledge Discovery from Data Streams*. Chapman and Hall (2010).
7. G. Ditzler, M. Roveri, C. Alippi, and R. Polikar, Learning in nonstationary environments: A survey, *IEEE Comp. Intell. Mag.* **10**(4), 12–25 (2015).
8. J. Stefanowski. Adaptive ensembles for evolving data streams - combining block-based and online solutions. In *Proc. 4th Int. Workshop New Frontiers Mining Complex Patterns*, vol. 9607, *Lecture Notes in Computer Science*, pp. 3–16, Springer (2015).
9. H. He and Y. Ma, eds., *Imbalanced Learning: Foundations, Algorithms, and Applications*. Wiley-IEEE Press (2013).
10. P. Branco, L. Torgo, and R. P. Ribeiro, A survey of predictive modelling under imbalanced distributions, *ACM Comput. Surv.* **49**(2), 31:1–31:50 (2016).
11. H. He and E. A. Garcia, Learning from imbalanced data, *IEEE Trans. Knowl. Data Eng.* **21**(9), 1263–1284 (2009).
12. S. Wang, L. L. Minku, and X. Yao. Dealing with multiple classes in online class imbalance learning. In *Proc. 25th Int. Joint Conf. Artificial Intelligence*, pp. 2118–2124, IJCAI/AAAI Press (2016).
13. A. Bifet, G. D. F. Morales, J. Read, G. Holmes, and B. Pfahringer. Efficient online evaluation of big data stream classifiers. In *Proc. 21st ACM SIGKDD Int. Conf. Knowl. Discovery Data Mining*, pp. 59–68, ACM (2015). ISBN 978-1-4503-3664-2.
14. D. Brzezinski and J. Stefanowski, Prequential AUC: Properties of the area under the ROC curve for data streams with concept drift, *Knowledge and Information Systems* (2017). doi: 10.1007/s10115-017-1022-8.

15. D. Brzezinski and J. Stefanowski. Stream classification. In eds. C. Sammut and G. I. Webb, *Encyclopedia of Machine Learning*. Springer (2016).
16. J. Gama, R. Sebastião, and P. P. Rodrigues, On evaluating stream learning algorithms, *Mach. Learn.* **90**(3), 317–346 (2013).
17. D. Brzezinski and J. Stefanowski, Reacting to different types of concept drift: The accuracy updated ensemble algorithm, *IEEE Trans. on Neural Netw. Learn. Syst.* **25**(1), 81–94 (2014).
18. J. Gama, P. Medas, G. Castillo, and P. P. Rodrigues. Learning with drift detection. In *Proc. 17th Brazilian Symp. Artificial Intelligence*, vol. 3171, *Lecture Notes in Computer Science*, pp. 286–295, Springer (2004).
19. A. Bifet and R. Gavaldà. Learning from time-changing data with adaptive windowing. In *Proc. 7th SIAM Int. Conf. Data Mining*, pp. 443–448, SIAM (2007).
20. A. Bifet, G. Holmes, B. Pfahringer, R. Kirkby, and R. Gavaldà. New ensemble methods for evolving data streams. In *Proc. 15th ACM SIGKDD Int. Conf. Knowl. Discovery Data Mining*, pp. 139–148, ACM (2009).
21. I. Zliobaite. Combining time and space similarity for small size learning under concept drift. In *Foundations of Intelligent Systems, Proc. 18th ISMIS Int. Symp.*, vol. 5722, *Lecture Notes in Computer Science*, pp. 412–421, Springer (2009).
22. S. Yoshida, K. Hatano, E. Takimoto, and M. Takeda, Adaptive online prediction using weighted windows, *IEICE Transactions.* **94-D**(10), 1917–1923 (2011).
23. P. Domingos and G. Hulten. Mining high-speed data streams. In *Proc. 6th ACM SIGKDD Int. Conf. Knowl. Discovery Data Mining*, pp. 71–80, ACM (2000).
24. W. N. Street and Y. Kim. A streaming ensemble algorithm (SEA) for large-scale classification. In *Proc. 7th ACM SIGKDD Int. Conf. Knowl. Discovery Data Mining*, pp. 377–382, ACM (2001).
25. H. Wang, W. Fan, P. S. Yu, and J. Han. Mining concept-drifting data streams using ensemble classifiers. In *Proc. 9th ACM SIGKDD Int. Conf. Knowl. Discovery Data Mining*, pp. 226–235, ACM (2003).
26. R. Elwell and R. Polikar, Incremental learning of concept drift in nonstationary environments, *IEEE Trans. Neural Netw.* **22**(10), 1517–1531 (Oct., 2011).
27. N. Littlestone and M. K. Warmuth, The weighted majority algorithm, *Inf. Comput.* **108**(2), 212–261 (1994).
28. N. C. Oza and S. J. Russell. Experimental comparisons of online and batch versions of bagging and boosting. In *Proc. 7th ACM SIGKDD Int. Conf. Knowl. Discovery Data Mining*, pp. 359–364, ACM (2001).
29. L. L. Minku and X. Yao, DDD: A new ensemble approach for dealing with concept drift, *IEEE Trans. Knowl. Data Eng.* **24**(4), 619–633 (2012).
30. J. Z. Kolter and M. A. Maloof, Dynamic weighted majority: An ensemble method for drifting concepts, *J. Mach. Learning Res.* **8**, 2755–2790 (2007).

31. D. Brzezinski and J. Stefanowski, Combining block-based and online methods in learning ensembles from concept drifting data streams, *Inf. Sci.* **265**, 50–67 (2014).

32. B. Krawczyk, L. L. Minku, J. Gama, J. Stefanowski, and M. Woniak. Ensemble learning for data stream analysis: A survey, *Inf. Fusion.* **37**, 132–156 (2017).

33. H. M. Gomes, J. P. Barddal, F. Enembreck, and A. Bifet. A survey on ensemble learning for data stream classification, *ACM Comput. Surv.* **50**(2), 23:1–23:36 (2017).

34. M. Kubat and S. Matwin. Addressing the curse of imbalanced training sets: one-side selection. In *Proc. 14th Int. Conf. Mach. Learn.*, pp. 179–186, Morgan Kaufmann (1997).

35. N. Japkowicz and M. Shah. *Evaluating Learning Algorithms: A Classification Perspective.* Cambridge University Press (2011).

36. G. Batista, R. C. Prati, and M. C. Monard. A study of the behavior of several methods for balancing machine learning training data, *ACM SIGKDD Explorations Newsletter.* **6**(1), 20–29 (2004).

37. K. Napierala. *Improving Rule Classifiers For Imbalanced Data.* PhD thesis, Poznan University of Technology (2013).

38. T. Jo and N. Japkowicz. Class imbalances versus small disjuncts, *SIGKDD Explorations.* **6**(1), 40–49 (2004).

39. V. Garcia, J. Sanchez, and R. Mollineda. An empirical study of the behavior of classifiers on imbalanced and overlapped data sets. In *Proc. 12th Iberoamerican Conf. Progress Pattern Recognition Image Analysis Applications*, vol. 4756, *Lecture Notes in Computer Science*, pp. 397–406, Springer (2007).

40. K. Napierala and J. Stefanowski. Identification of different types of minority class examples in imbalanced data. In *Proc. Conf. Hybrid Artifficial Intelligence Systems*, vol. 7209, *Lecture Notes in Computer Science*, pp. 139–150, Springer (2012).

41. K. Napierala and J. Stefanowski, Types of minority class examples and their influence on learning classifiers from imbalanced data, *J. Intell. Inf. Syst.* **46**(3), 563–597 (2016).

42. J. Stefanowski. Overlapping, rare examples and class decomposition in learning classifiers from imbalanced data. In eds. S. Ramanna, L. C. Jain, and R. J. Howlett, *Emerging Paradigms in Machine Learning*, vol. 13, *Smart Innovation, Systems and Technologies*, pp. 277–306. Springer (2013).

43. N. Japkowicz and S. Stephen, The class imbalance problem: A systematic study, *Intell. Data Anal.* **6**(5), 429–449 (2002).

44. R. C. Prati, G. Batista, and M. C. Monard. Learning with class skews and small disjuncts. In *Proc. of SBIA'04*, vol. 3171, *Lecture Notes in Computer Science*, pp. 296–306, Springer (2004).

45. K. Napierala, J. Stefanowski, and S. Wilk. Learning from imbalanced data in presence of noisy and borderline examples. In *Proc. of 7th Int. Conf. Rough Sets and Current Trends in Computing*, vol. 6086, *Lecture Notes in Artifficial Intelligence*, pp. 158–167, Springer (2010).

46. N. V. Chawla, K. W. Bowyer, L. O. Hall, and W. P. Kegelmeyer, SMOTE: synthetic minority over-sampling technique, *J. Artif. Int. Res.* **16**, 321–357 (2002).

47. M. Galar, A. Fernandez, E. Barrenechea, H. Bustince, and F. Herrera. A review on ensembles for the class imbalance problem: Bagging-, boosting-, and hybrid-based approaches, *IEEE Trans. Systems Man Cybernetics, Part C.* **42**(4), 463–484 (2012).

48. L. A and Z. Zhu. Ensemble methods for class imbalance learning. In eds. H. He and M. Yungian, *Imbalanced Learning. Foundations, Algorithms and Applications*, pp. 61–82. Wiley (2013).

49. S. Hido and H. Kashima. Roughly balanced bagging for imbalanced data. In *Proc. of 8th SIAM Int. Conf. Data Mining*, pp. 143–152, SIAM (2008).

50. M. Lango and J. Stefanowski. Multi-class and feature selection extensions of roughly balanced bagging for imbalanced data, *Journal of Intelligent Information Systems*. pp. 1–31 (2017). doi: 10.1007/s10844-017-0446-7.

51. J. Blaszczynski and J. Stefanowski, Neighbourhood sampling in bagging for imbalanced data, *Neurocomputing*. **150**, 184–203 (2015).

52. J. Gao, B. Ding, W. Fan, J. Han, and P. S. Yu. Classifying data streams with skewed class distributions and concept drifts, *IEEE Internet Computing*. **12** (6), 37–49 (2008).

53. S. Chen and H. He. SERA: selectively recursive approach towards nonstationary imbalanced stream data mining. In *Int. Joint Conf. Neural Networks*, pp. 522–529, IEEE Computer Society (2009).

54. S. Chen, H. He, K. Li, and S. Desai. MuSeRA: Multiple selectively recursive approach towards imbalanced stream data mining. In *Proc. 2010 Int. Joint Conf. Neural Networks*, pp. 1–8, IEEE (2010).

55. S. Chen and H. He. Towards incremental learning of concept drift from imbalanced data streams, *Evolving Systems*. **2**(1), 35–50 (2011).

56. R. Lichtenwalter and N. V. Chawla. Adaptive methods for classification in arbitrarily imbalanced and drifting data streams. In *Revised Selected Papers Int, Workshop New Frontiers Applied Data Mining*, vol. 5669, *Lecture Notes in Computer Science*, pp. 53–75, Springer (2009).

57. T. R. Hoens and N. V. Chawla. Learning in non-stationary environments with class imbalance. In *Proc. 18th ACM SIGKDD Int. Conf. Knowl. Discovery Data Mining*, pp. 168–176, ACM (2012).

58. G. Ditzler and R. Polikar, Incremental learning of concept drift from streaming imbalanced data, *IEEE Trans. Knowl. Data Eng.* **25**(10), 2283–2301 (2013).

59. J. Zhang, X. Hu, Y. Zhang, and P.-P. Li. An efficient ensemble method for classifying skewed data streams. In *Proc. 7th Int. Conf. Intelligent Computing*, vol. 6840, *Lecture Notes in Computer Science*, pp. 144–151, Springer (2011).

60. H. Nguyen, E. Cooper, and K. Kamei. Online learning from imbalanced data streams. In *Proc. 2011 Int. Conf. Soft Computing Pattern Recognition*, pp. 347–352, IEEE (2011).

61. S. Wang, L. L. Minku, and X. Yao. A learning framework for online class imbalance learning. In *Proc. IEEE Symp. Computational Intelligence Ensemble Learning*, pp. 36–45, IEEE (2013).
62. S. Wang, L. L. Minku, and X. Yao, Resampling-based ensemble methods for online class imbalance learning, *IEEE Trans. Knowl. Data Eng.* **27**(5), 1356–1368 (2015).
63. A. Ghazikhani, R. Monsefi, and H. S. Yazdi, Ensemble of online neural networks for non-stationary and imbalanced data streams, *Neurocomputing.* **122**, 535–544 (2013).
64. B. Mirza, Z. Lin, and N. Liu, Ensemble of subset online sequential extreme learning machine for class imbalance and concept drift, *Neurocomputing.* **149**, 316–329 (2015).
65. A. Bifet, G. Holmes, R. Kirkby, and B. Pfahringer, MOA: Massive Online Analysis, *J. Mach. Learn. Res.* **11**, 1601–1604 (2010).
66. T. Theeramunkong, B. Kijsirikul, N. Cercone, and T. B. Ho. PAKDD data mining competition (2009).
67. D. Brzezinski and J. Stefanowski, Combining block-based and online methods in learning ensembles from concept drifting data streams, *Inform. Sciences.* **265**, 50–67 (2014).
68. D. Brzezinski and J. Stefanowski. Prequential AUC for classifier evaluation and drift detection in evolving data streams. In *Proc. 3rd Int. Workshop New Frontiers Mining Complex Patterns*, vol. 8983, *Lecture Notes in Computer Science*, pp. 87–101, Springer (2015).

Chapter 4

Consensus Learning for Sequence Data

Andreas Nienkötter* and Xiaoyi Jiang†

Faculty of Mathematics and Computer Science, University of Münster
Einsteinstrasse 62, D-48149 Münster, Germany
*a.nienkoetter@uni-muenster.de
†xjiang@uni-muenster.de

Learning a prototype from a set of given objects is a core problem in machine learning, data mining, and pattern recognition. A commonly used approach to consensus learning is to formulate it as an optimization problem in terms of generalized median computation. Sequential data can be effectively represented by strings. In this chapter we discuss how the median concept can be applied to strings. We introduce the notion of median string and provide related theoretical results. Then, we give a brief review of algorithmic procedures for computing median strings. Experimental results will be reported to compare some of the shown algorithms.

1. Introduction

Learning a prototype from a set of given objects is a core problem in machine learning, data mining, and pattern recognition and has numerous applications.[1] Prototypes are often used to index large-size data so that queries can be efficiently answered by only considering those prototypes. Another example is multiple classifier combination, where a change of algorithm parameters or the use of different algorithms can lead to distinct results, each with small diverse errors. Consensus methods produce a final result which best represents the different results and thus removes errors and outliers in the input ensemble.

Strings provide a simple and yet powerful representation scheme for sequential data. In particular time series can be effectively represented by strings. A large number of operations and algorithms have been proposed to deal with strings.[2-7] Some of them are inherent to the special nature of strings such as the shortest common superstring and the longest common substring, while others are adapted from other domains.

String algorithms have found numerous applications in a broad range of fields including computer vision, language processing, speech recognition, and molecular biology. In data mining, clustering and machine learning, a typical task is to represent a set of (similar) objects by means of a single prototype. In particular, a commonly used approach to consensus learning is to formulate it as an optimization problem in terms of generalized median computation. This median concept is useful in various contexts. It represents a fundamental quantity in statistics. In sensor fusion, multi-sensory measurements of some quantity are averaged to produce the best estimate. Averaging the results of several classifiers is used in multiple classifier systems in order to achieve more reliable classifications. Interesting applications of the median concept have been demonstrated in dealing with rankings,[8] 3D rigid structures,[9] rotation,[10] clustering,[11] graphs,[12] shape,[13] atlas construction,[14] binary feature maps,[15] geometric features (points, lines, or 3D frames),[16] brain models,[17] anatomical structures,[18] and facial images.[19] In this chapter we discuss the adaptation of the median concept to the domain of strings.

This chapter is an updated version of the previous paper[20] including recent developments. The outline of the chapter is as follows. We first formally introduce the median string problem in Section 2 and provide some related theoretical results in Section 3. Sections 4 and 5 are devoted to algorithmic procedures for computing set median and generalized median strings. In Section 6 we report experimental results to demonstrate the median concept and to compare some of the considered algorithms. Finally, some discussions conclude this chapter.

2. Median String Problem

Assuming an alphabet Σ of symbols, a string x is simply a sequence of symbols from Σ, i.e., $x = x_1 x_2 \ldots x_n$, where $x_i \in \Sigma$ for $i = 1, \ldots, n$. Given the space U of all strings over Σ, we need a distance function $d(p, q)$ to measure the dissimilarity between two strings $p, q \in U$. Let S be a set of N strings from U. The essential information of S is captured by a string $\bar{p} \in U$ that minimizes the sum of distances of $\bar{p}$ to all strings from S, also called the consensus error $E_S(p)$:

$$\bar{p} = \arg \min_{p \in U} E_S(p), \quad \text{where } E_S(p) = \sum_{q \in S} d(p, q).$$

The string $\bar{p}$ is called a *generalized median* of S. If the search is constrained to the given set S, the resultant string

$$\hat{p} = \arg\min_{p \in S} E_S(p)$$

is called a *set median* of S. For a given set S, neither the generalized median nor the set median is necessarily unique. This definition was introduced by Kohonen.[21] Note that different terminology has been used in the literature. In some works the set median string and the generalized median string are termed *center string* and *Steiner string*,[4] respectively, while in others the generalized median was called *consensus sequence*.[22]

A different possibility is mentioned by Kohonen[21] too. This is the parallel of mean from elementary statistics. Here we would like to search for p' that minimizes

$$\sum_{q \in S} d^2(p', q).$$

Martinez-Hinarejos *et al.*[23] returned to this definition and investigated the possibility of using mean instead of median. Generally, this variant can be interpreted as a special instance of the generalized median problem using d^2 as the distance function.

Several string distance functions have been proposed in the literature. The most popular one is doubtlessly the Levenshtein edit distance. Let $A = a_1 a_2 \ldots a_n$ and $B = b_1 b_2 \ldots b_m$ be two words over Σ. The Levenshtein edit distance $d(A, B)$ is defined in terms of elementary edit operations which are required to transform A into B. Usually, three different types of edit operations are considered, namely (1) substitution of a symbol $a \in A$ by a symbol $b \in B, a \neq b$, (2) insertion of a symbol $a \in \Sigma$ in B, and (3) deletion of a symbol $a \in A$. Symbolically, we write $a \to b$ for a substitution, $\varepsilon \to a$ for an insertion, and $a \to \varepsilon$ for a deletion. To model the fact that some distortions may be more likely than others, costs of edit operations, $c(a \to b)$, $c(\varepsilon \to a)$, and $c(a \to \varepsilon)$, are introduced. Let $s = l_1 l_2 \ldots l_k$ be a sequence of edit operations transforming A into B. We define the cost of this sequence by $c(s) = \sum_{i=1}^{k} c(l_i)$. Given two strings A and B, the Levenshtein edit distance is given by $d(A, B) = \min\{c(s) \mid s:$ sequence of edit operations transforming A into B $\}$. To illustrate the Levenshtein edit distance, let us consider two words $A = median$ and $B = mean$ built on the English alphabet. Examples of sequences of edit operations transforming A into B are:

- $s_1 = d \rightarrow a, i \rightarrow n, a \rightarrow \varepsilon, n \rightarrow \varepsilon$
- $s_2 = d \rightarrow a, i \rightarrow \varepsilon, a \rightarrow \varepsilon$
- $s_3 = d \rightarrow \varepsilon, i \rightarrow \varepsilon$

Under the edit cost $c(a \rightarrow \varepsilon) = c(\varepsilon \rightarrow a) = c(a \rightarrow b) = 1, a \neq b$, s_3 represents the optimal sequence with the minimum total cost 2 for transforming *median* into *mean* among all possible transformations. Therefore, we observe $d(median, mean) = 2$. The most popular algorithm to compute the Levenshtein distance was proposed by Wagner and Fisher[24] by means of dynamic programming. Since then, many improvements or other algorithms have appeared.[2,4,5]

Further string distance functions are known from the literature, for instance, normalized edit distance,[25] Hamming distance, maximum posterior probability distance,[21] feature distance,[21] and others.[26,27] The Levenshtein edit distance is by far the most popular one. Actually, some of the algorithms we discuss later are tightly coupled to this particular distance function.

3. Theoretical Results

In this section we summarize some theoretical results related to median strings. The generalized median is a more general concept and usually a better representation of the given strings than the set median. From a practical point of view, the set median can be regarded an approximate solution of the generalized median. As such it may serve as the start for an iterative refinement process to find more accurate approximations. Interestingly, we have the following result (see Gusfield[4] for a proof):

Theorem 1. *Assume that the string distance function satisfies the triangle inequality. Then $E_S(\hat{p})/E_S(\bar{p}) \leq 2 - 2/|S|$.*

That is, the set median has a consensus error relative to S that is at most $2 - 2/|S|$ times the consensus error of the generalized median string.

Independent of the distance function we can always find the set median of N strings by means of $\frac{1}{2}N(N-1)$ pairwise distance computations. This computational burden can be further reduced by making use of special properties of the distance function (e.g., metric) or resorting to approximate procedures. Section 4 will present examples of these approaches.

Compared to set median strings, the computation of generalized median strings represents a much more demanding task. This is due to the huge search space which is substantially larger than that for determining the set median string. This intuitive understanding of the computational complexity is supported by the following theoretical results. Under the two conditions:

- every edit operation has cost one, i.e., $c(a \to b) = c(\varepsilon \to a) = c(a \to \varepsilon) = 1$,
- the alphabet is not of fixed size,

de la Higuera and Casacuberta[28] proved that computing the generalized median string is NP-hard for an unbounded alphabet. Sim and Park[29] proved that the problem is NP-hard for finite alphabet and for a metric distance matrix. Furthermore, Nicolas and Rivals showed the same hardness even for a binary alphabet.[30] Another result comes from computational biology. The optimal evolutionary tree problem there turns out to be equivalent to the problem of computing generalized median strings if the tree structure is a star (a tree with $n+1$ nodes, n of them being leaves). Wang and Jiang[31] proved that in this particular case the optimal evolutionary tree problem is NP-hard. The distance function used is problem dependent and does not even satisfy the triangle inequality. All these theoretical results indicate the inherent difficulty in finding generalized median strings. Not surprisingly, the algorithms we will discuss in Section 5 are either exponential or approximate.

4. Fast Computation of Set Median Strings

The naive computation of set median requires $O(N^2)$ distance computations. Considering the relatively high computational cost of each individual string distance, this straightforward approach may not be appropriate, especially in the case of a large number of strings. The problem of fast set median search can be tackled by making use of properties of metric distance functions or developing approximate algorithms. Several solutions[32,33] have been suggested for fast set median search in arbitrary spaces. They apply to the domain of strings as well.

4.1. *Exact Set Median Search in Metric Spaces*

In many applications the underlying string distance function is a metric which satisfies:

(1) $d(p,q) \geq 0$ and $d(p,q) = 0$ if and only if $p = q$,

(2) $d(p,q) = d(q,p)$,
(3) $d(p,q) + d(q,r) \geq d(p,r)$.

A property of metrics is:

$$|d(p,r) - d(r,q)| \leq d(p,q), \; \forall p,q,r \in S, \tag{1}$$

which can be utilized to reduce the number of string distance computations.

The approach proposed by Juan and Vidal[32] partitions the input set S into subsets S_u (used), S_e (eliminated), and S_a (alive). The set S_a keeps track of those strings that have not been fully evaluated yet; initially $S_a = S$. A lower bound $g(p)$ is computed for each string p in S_a, i.e., the consensus error of p satisfies:

$$E_S(p) = \sum_{q \in S} d(p,q) \geq g(p).$$

Clearly, strings with small g values are potentially better candidates for set median. For this reason the string p with the smallest $g(p)$ value among all strings in S_a is transferred from S_a to S_u. Then, the consensus error $E_S(p)$ is computed and, if necessary, the current best median candidate p is updated. Then, the lower bound g is computed for all strings that are alive, and those whose g is not smaller than $E_S(p)$ are moved from S_a to S_e. They will not be considered as median candidates any longer. This process is repeated until S_a becomes empty.

In each iteration, the consensus error for p with the smallest g value is computed by:

$$E_S(p) = \sum_{q \in S_u} d(p,q) + \sum_{q \in S_e \cup (S_a - \{p\})} d(p,q).$$

Using (1) the term $d(p,q)$ in the second summation is estimated by:

$$d(p,q) \geq |d(p,r) - d(r,q)|, \forall r \in S_u.$$

Taking all strings of S_u into account, we obtain the lower bound:

$$E_S(p) \geq \sum_{q \in S_u} d(p,q) + \sum_{q \in S_e \cup (S_a - \{p\})} \max_{r \in S_u} |d(p,r) - d(r,q)| = g(p). \tag{2}$$

The critical point here is to see that all the distances in this lower bound are concerned with p and strings from S_u, and were therefore already computed before. When strings in S_a are eliminated (moved to S_u), their consensus errors need not to be computed in future. This fact results in saving of distance computations. In addition to (2), two other lower bounds within the same algorithmic framework are given by Juan and Vidal.[32] They differ in the resulting ratio of the number of distance computations and the remaining overhead, with the lower bound (2) requiring the smallest amount of distance computations.

Ideally, the distance function is desired to be a metric, in order to match the human intuition of similarity. The triangle inequality excludes the case in which $d(p,r)$ and $d(r,q)$ are both small, but $d(p,q)$ is very large. In practice, however, there may exist distance functions which do not satisfy the triangle inequality. To judge the suitability of these distance functions, other works[34] suggest quasimetrics with a relaxed triangle inequality. Instead of the strict triangle inequality, the relation:

$$d(p,r) + d(r,q) \geq \frac{d(p,q)}{1+\varepsilon}$$

is required now. Here ε is a small nonnegative constant. As long as ε is not very large, the relaxed triangle inequality still retains the human intuition of similarity. Note that the strict triangle inequality is a special case with $\varepsilon = 0$. The fast set median search procedure[32] sketched above easily extends to quasi-metrics. In this case the relationship (1) is replaced by:

$$d(p,q) \geq \max\left(\frac{d(p,r)}{1+\varepsilon} - d(q,r), \frac{d(q,r)}{1+\varepsilon} - d(p,r)\right), \ \forall p,r,q \in S$$

which can be used in the same manner to establish a lower bound $g(p)$.

4.2. *Approximate Set Median Search in Arbitrary Spaces*

Another approach to fast set median search makes no assumption on the distance function and therefore covers non-metrics as well. The idea of this approximate algorithm is simple. Instead of computing the sum of distances of each string to all the other strings of S to select the best one, only a subset of S is used to obtain an estimation of the consensus error.[33] The algorithm first calculates such estimations and then calculates the exact consensus errors only for strings that have low estimations.

This approximate algorithm proceeds in two steps. First, a random subset S_r of N_r strings is selected from S. For each string p of S, the consensus error $E_{S_r}(p)$ relative to S_r is computed and serves as an estimation of the consensus error $E_S(p)$. In the second step N_t strings with the lowest consensus error estimations are chosen. The exact consensus error $E_S(p)$ is computed for the N_t strings and the string with the minimum $E_S(p)$ is regarded the (approximate) set median string of S.

5. Computation of Generalized Median Strings

While the set median problem is characterized by selecting one particular member out of a given set of strings, the computation of generalized median strings is inherently constructive. The theoretical results from Section 3 about computational complexity indicate the fundamental difficulties we are faced with. In the following we describe various algorithms for computing generalized median strings. Not surprisingly, they are either of exponential complexity or approximate.

5.1. *An Exact Algorithm and its Variants*

An algorithm for the exact computation of generalized median strings under the Levenshtein distance is given by Kruskal.[35] Let ε be the empty string and $\Sigma' = \Sigma \cup \{\varepsilon\}$ the extended alphabet. We define:

$$\delta(r_1, r_2, \ldots, r_N) = \min_{v \in \Sigma'} [c(v \to r_1) + c(v \to r_2) + \cdots + c(v \to r_N)].$$

The operator δ can be interpreted as a voting function, as it determines the best value v at a given stage of computation. Finding an optimal value of v requires an exhaustive search over Σ' in the most general case, but in practice the cost function is often simple such that a shortcut can be taken and the choice of the optimal v is not costly.

Having defined δ this way, the generalized median string can be computed by means of dynamic programming in an N-dimensional array, similarly to string edit distance computation.[24] For the sake of notational simplicity, we only discuss the case $N = 3$. Assume the three input strings be $u_1 u_2 \ldots u_l$, $v_1 v_2 \ldots v_m$, and $w_1 w_2 \ldots w_n$. A three-dimensional distance table of dimension $l \times m \times n$ is constructed as follows:

initialization:+ $d_{0,0,0} = 0$;
iteration:

$$d_{i,j,k} = \min \begin{cases} d_{i-1,j-1,k-1} & + \delta(u_i, v_j, w_k) \\ d_{i-1,j-1,k} & + \delta(u_i, v_j, \varepsilon) \\ d_{i-1,j,k-1} & + \delta(u_i, \varepsilon, w_k) \\ d_{i-1,j,k} & + \delta(u_i, \varepsilon, \varepsilon) \\ d_{i,j-1,k-1} & + \delta(\varepsilon, v_j, w_k) \\ d_{i,j-1,k} & + \delta(\varepsilon, v_j, \varepsilon) \\ d_{i,j,k-1} & + \delta(\varepsilon, \varepsilon, w_k) \end{cases} \left\{ \begin{array}{l} 0 \le i \le l \\ 0 \le j \le m \\ 0 \le k \le n \end{array} \right\}$$

end: if $(i = l) \wedge (j = m) \wedge (k = n)$

The computation requires $O(lmn)$ time and space. The path in the distance table that leads from $d_{0,0,0}$ to $d_{l,m,n}$ defines the generalized median string $\bar{p}$ with $d_{l,m,n}$ being the consensus error $E_S(p)$. Note that a generalization to arbitrary N is straightforward. If the strings of S are of length $O(n)$, both the time and space complexity amounts to $O(n^N)$ in this case.

Despite of its mathematical elegance the exact algorithm above is impractical because of the exponential complexity. There have been efforts to shorten the computation time using heuristics or domain-specific knowledge. One such approach assumes that the string of S be quite similar.[22] Under reasonable constraints on the cost function ($c(a \to \varepsilon) = c(\varepsilon \to a) = 1$ and $c(a \to b)$ nonnegative), the generalized median string $\bar{p}$ satisfies $E_S(p) \leq k$ with k being a small number. In this case the optimal dynamic programming path must be close to the main diagonal in the distance table. Therefore only part of the N-dimensional table needs to be considered.[22] The asymptotic time complexity of this restricted search is $O(nk^N)$. While this remains exponential, k is typically much smaller than n, resulting in a substantial speedup compared to the full search of the original algorithm.[35] An integer linear programming formulation based on both the original dynamic programming algorithm and the improved version was provided by Zou *et al.*[36]

We may also use any domain-specific knowledge to limit the search space. An example is the approach in the context of classifier combination for handwritten sentence recognition.[37] An ensemble of classifiers provide multiple classification results of a scanned text. Then, the consensus string is expected to yield the best overall recognition performance. The input strings from the individual classifiers are associated with additional information of position, i.e., the location of each individual word in a sequence of handwritten words. Obviously, it is very unlikely that a word at the beginning of a sequence corresponds to a word at the end of another sequence. More generally, only words at a similar position in the text image are meaningful candidates for being matched to each other. Marti and Bunke [37] make use of this observation in the above case to exclude a large portion of the full N-dimensional search space from consideration.

5.2. *Approximate Algorithms*

Because of the NP-hardness of generalized median string computation, efforts have been undertaken to develop approximate approaches which provide suboptimal solutions in reasonable time. In this section we will discuss several algorithms of this class.

Algorithm 1 General framework of greedy algorithms

$\bar{p}_0 = \varepsilon$
for $(l = 1; ; l + +)$ **do**
$\quad a_l = \arg\min\limits_{a \in \Sigma} E_S(\bar{p}_{l-1}a)$
$\quad \bar{p}_l = \bar{p}_{l-1}a_l$
$\quad$ **if** termination criterion fulfilled **then**
$\quad\quad$ **return** prefix of $\bar{p}_l$
$\quad$ **end if**
end for

5.2.1. *Greedy Algorithms*

The following algorithm was proposed by Casacuberta and de Antonio.[38] Starting from an empty string, a greedy algorithm constructs an approximate generalized median string $\bar{p}$ symbol by symbol. When we are going to generate the l-th symbol $a_l(l \geq 1)$, the substring $a_1 \ldots a_{l-1}(\varepsilon$ for $l = 1)$ has already been determined. Then, each symbol from Σ is considered as a candidate for a_l. All the candidates are evaluated and the final decision of a_l is made by selecting the best candidate. The process is continued until a termination criterion is fulfilled.

A general framework of greedy algorithms is given in Algorithm 1. There are several possible choices for the termination criterion and the prefix. The greedy algorithm proposed by Casacuberta and de Antonio[38] stops the iterative construction process when $E_S(\bar{p}_l) > E_S(\bar{p}_{l-1})$. Then, $\bar{p}_{l-1}$ is regarded the approximate generalized median string. Alternatively, Kruzslicz[39] suggests the termination criterion $l = \max\limits_{p \in S} |p|$. The output is the prefix of $\bar{p}_l$ with the smallest consensus error relative to S. For both variants a suitable data structure [38] enables a time complexity of $O(n^2 N|\Sigma|)$ for the Levenshtein distance. The space complexity amounts to $O(nN|\Sigma|)$.

In the general framework in Algorithm 1 nothing is stated about how to select a_l if there exist multiple symbols from Σ with the same value of $E_S(\bar{p}_{l-1}a)$. Besides a simple random choice, the history of the selection process can be taken into account to make a more reliable decision.[39]

5.2.2. *Evolutionary weighted mean approach*

The evolutionary weighted mean framework by Franek and Jiang[40] is a method to compute the generalized median of arbitrary objects, and therefore can be applied to strings as well.

It is motivated by the lower bound of the generalized median by Jiang *et al.*[12] The consensus error is defined as (N even):

$$E_S(\bar{p}) = \sum_{q \in S} d(\bar{p}, q)$$

$$= (d(\bar{p}, p_1) + d(\bar{p}, p_2)) + \cdots + (d(\bar{p}, p_{N-1}) + d(\bar{p}, p_N)).$$

Applying the triangle inequality

$$d(p_i, \bar{p}) + d(\bar{p}, p_j) \geq d(p_i, p_j)$$

to each pair of distance calculations leads to

$$E_S(\bar{p}) \geq d(p_1, p_2) + d(p_3, p_4) + \cdots + d(p_{N-1}, p_N),$$

which is true for each permutation of p_i. Therefore,

$$E_S(\bar{p}) \geq \max\{d(p_1, p_2) + \cdots + d(p_{N-1}, p_N) \tag{3}$$
$$\mid (p_1, p_2), \ldots, (p_{N-1}, p_N) \text{ is a partition of } S\}.$$

If the lower bound is reached, then the triangle inequality becomes an equality. This can be imagined as the generalized median lying on the intersection point of the lines between each pair. This is illustrated in vector space in Figure 1(a).

This intersection point can be approximated using the so called weighted mean of the object pairs. The weighted mean $\tilde{p}$ between two objects p_i and p_j at ratio α is defined as

$$d(p_i, \tilde{p}) = \alpha \cdot d(p_i, p_j), \quad d(\tilde{p}, p_j) = (1 - \alpha)d(p_i, p_j). \tag{4}$$

Geometrically, the weighted mean can be seen as a linear interpolation between two objects. A function to compute the weighted mean can often be derived from the distance function itself. The Levenshtein distance for example can be extended to return a list of edit operations to transform the first string into the second. A weighted mean is then computed by applying edit operations one after another until the distance of $d(p_i, \tilde{p})$ is at least $\alpha \cdot d(p_i, p_j)$.[41]

If the lines between object pairs do not intersect, then the weighted mean can be used to compute an approximation of the generalized median, as illustrated in Figure 1(b).

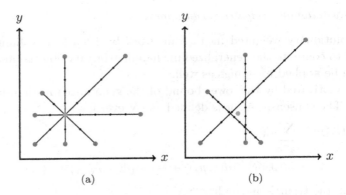

Fig. 1.   Generalized median in two-dimensional vector space. Red points: initial objects. Green point: generalized median. black points: weighted means. (a) Generalized median is on the intersection between pairs of initial points. (b) Lines between pairs do not intersect in a point.

Algorithm 2 Evolutionary weighted mean framework

Given a string set $S = \{p_1, \ldots, p_N\}$
Compute a partition of S into pairs (p_{i1}, p_{i2}) to maximize Equation (3)
for each pair (p_{i1}, p_{i2}) **do**
    Compute w weighted means $\tilde{p}_i$ by using $\alpha = \frac{i \cdot d(p_{i1}, p_{i2})}{w+1}$, $i = 1, \ldots, w$
    $\tilde{p} = \min_{i=1,\ldots,w}\{E_S(\tilde{p}_i)\}$
    $S = S \cup \{\tilde{p}\}$
end for
Delete the strings from S with the worst $E_S(p)$ until $|S| \leq N_{max}$.
if the lower bound is matched or convergence is achieved **then**
    return the string from S with the lowest $E_S(p)$
else
    Restart the algorithm with the current set S
end if

The evolutionary weighted mean framework shown in Algorithm 2 uses these properties to compute an approximation of the generalized median. First, the objects are divided into sets that maximize the pairwise distances. Then for each pair of objects a number of weighted means are calculated and the best one is added to the set. In the end, objects with the highest $E_S(p)$ are discarded to prevent the set from growing too much.

5.2.3. *Vector space embedding*

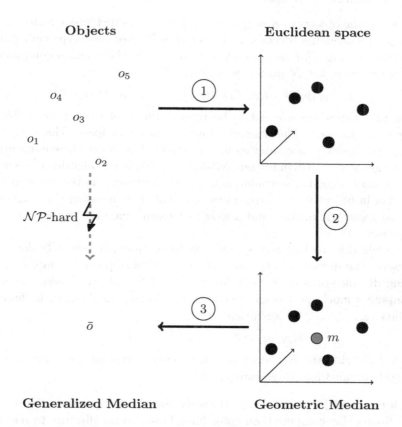

Fig. 2. Overview of the vector space embedding framework. Direct calculation is often NP-hard, depending on the distance function. (1) Embed objects into vector space. (2) Compute the median in vector space. (3) Reconstruct a median object from vectors.

Another method to compute the generalized median of arbitrary objects is vector space embedding.[42] The idea of this algorithm is to not compute the generalized median of the objects directly, but instead compute it in a vector space, where this task is much more easily solved. As can be seen in Figure 2, this process can be divided into three steps:

(1) Embed objects into a vector space.
(2) Compute the generalized median in vector space.

(3) Reconstruct the median in object space based on its position and neighborhood in vector space.

First, the objects in $S = \{p_1, \ldots, p_N\}$ are embedded into a vector space using an embedding function φ. Ferrer *et al.*[42] used prototype embedding for this purpose. For each object p_i in the set S, this method computes a vector x_i using $k \leq N$ prototype objects $\{P_1, \ldots, P_k\} \subset S$:

$$x_i = \varphi(p_i) = (d(p_i, P_1), d(p_i, P_2), \ldots, d(p_i, P_k)) \in \mathbb{R}^k.$$

The prototypes are selected to be representative of the set, often by k-means clustering.[42] The generalized median in vector space, which is called geometric median, is computed in the second step. Since the computation of the geometric median is again NP-hard, the Weiszfeld algorithm[43] is used to calculate a good approximation in a very short time. In the last step, the median in object space is reconstructed. This is done using the neighbors of the geometric median and a weighted mean function[44] as described in Equation (4).

While this method is easy and fast to compute, it generally does not preserve the distances very well. Therefore, this step can be improved by using distance-preserving embedding methods[45] instead. These methods compute a much more accurate embedding in reasonable time, by finding points $x_1, \ldots, x_N \in \mathbb{R}^k$ such that

$$\delta(p_i, p_j) \approx \delta_e(x_i, x_j), \ \forall 1 \leq i, j \leq N$$

with $\delta_e()$ being the Euclidean distance between two points. They can be roughly divided into three categories:[45]

Reference object methods: Methods like FastMap, MetricMap and SparseMap compute their embedding based on the distance to selected objects from the original set, similar to prototype embedding

Error minimization methods: These methods propose an error function on the embedding vectors. The vectors are optimized using these methods to form an accurate embedding, often by gradient descent. Examples are MDS, Sammon Mapping, CCA and t-SNE.

Neighborhood graph methods: Methods like MVU, LLE and IsoMap construct a neighborhood graph for the objects and base their embedding on this graph.

Each of these methods can be used instead of the prototype embedding for an often more accurate result, thereby improving the median computation.[45]

By using the Levenshtein edit distance and the weighted mean function described in Section 5.2.2, this framework can be applied to compute very accurate generalized medians of strings.[45]

5.2.4. *Perturbation-based Iterative Refinement*

The results of the algorithms above as well as the set median represent an approximation of the true generalized median string of a set. This approximate solution $\bar{p}$ can be further improved by an iterative process of systematic perturbations. The idea was first suggested by Kohonen,[21] but without algorithmic details. A concrete algorithm for realizing systematic perturbations is given in .[46] For each position i, the following operations are performed:

(1) Build perturbation
  - Substitution: replace the i-th symbol of $\bar{p}$ by each symbol of Σ in turn and choose the resulting string x with the smallest consensus error relative to S.
  - Insertion: insert each symbol of Σ in turn at the i-th position of $\bar{p}$ and choose the resulting string y with the smallest consensus error relative to S.
  - Deletion: delete the i-th symbol of $\bar{p}$ to generate z.
(2) Replace $\bar{p}$ by the one from $\{\bar{p}, x, y, z\}$ with the smallest consensus error relative to S.

For the Levenshtein distance one global iteration that handles all positions of the initial $\bar{p}$ needs $O(n^3 N |\Sigma|)$ time. The process is repeated until there is no more improvement possible.

Alternative methods to select the best perturbed string are also possible. Abreu and Rico-Juan[47] for example rank each possible edit operation on $\bar{p}$ by how much $E_S(\bar{p})$ is affected by it, and iteratively apply the best operation until there is no more improvement.

5.3. *Dynamic Computation of Generalized Median Strings*

In a dynamic context we are faced with the situation of a steady arrival of new data items, represented by strings. At each point of time, t, the set S^t of existing strings is incremented by a new string, resulting in S^{t+1}, and its generalized median string is to be computed. Doubtlessly, a trivial solution consists in applying any of the approaches discussed above to S^{t+1}.

By doing this however, we compute the generalized median string of S^{t+1} from scratch without utilizing any knowledge about S^t, in particular its generalized median string. All algorithms for computing generalized median strings are of such a static nature and thus not optimal in a dynamic context. Jiang *et al.*[48] propose a genuinely dynamic approach, in which the update scheme only considers the generalized median string of S^t together with the new data item, but not the individual members of S^t.

The inspiration for the algorithm comes from a fundamental fact in real space. Under the distance function $d(p_i, p_j) = (p_i - p_j) \cdot (p_i - p_j)$, i.e., the squared Euclidean distance of p_i and p_j, the generalized median of a given set $S^t = \{p_1, p_2, \ldots, p_t\}$ of t points is the well-known mean:

$$\bar{p}^t = \frac{1}{t} \cdot \sum_{i=1}^{t} p_i.$$

When an additional point p_{t+1} is added to S_t, the resultant new set $S^{t+1} = S^t \cup \{p_{t+1}\}$ has the generalized median

$$\bar{p}^{t+1} = \frac{1}{t+1} \cdot \sum_{i=1}^{t+1} p_i = \frac{t}{t+1} \cdot \bar{p}^t + \frac{1}{t+1} \cdot p_{t+1},$$

which is the weighted mean of $\bar{p}^t$ and p_{t+1} satisfying

$$d(\bar{p}^{t+1}, \bar{p}^t) = \frac{1}{t+1} \cdot d(\bar{p}^t, p_{t+1})$$

$$d(\bar{p}^{t+1}, p_{t+1}) = \frac{t}{t+1} \cdot d(\bar{p}^t, p_{t+1}).$$

On a heuristic basis the special case in real space can be extended to the domain of strings. Given a set $S^t = \{p_1, p_2, \ldots, p_t\}$ of t strings and its generalized median $\bar{p}^t$, the generalized median of a new set $S^{t+1} = S^t \cup \{p_{t+1}\}$ is estimated by a weighted mean of $\bar{p}^t$ and p_{t+1} with a ratio $\alpha \in [0,1]$, in the same manner as in Section 5.2.2. In real space α takes the value $\frac{1}{t+1}$. For strings, however, we have no possibility to specify α in advance. Therefore, we resort to a search procedure. Remember that our goal is to find $\bar{p}^{t+1}$ that minimizes the consensus error relative to S^{t+1}. To determine the optimal α value a series of α values $0, \frac{1}{k}, \ldots, \frac{k-1}{k}, 1$ is probed and the α value that results in the smallest consensus error is chosen.

6. Experimental Evaluation

In this section we report some experimental results of several methods described above. The used datasets are shown in Table 1. The Copenhagen

Table 1. Evaluated datasets

Dataset	Type	Number of Sets	Number of Strings in each Set	Number of Symbols
CCD	real	22	100	11
Darwin	artificial	21	40	52
MSNBC	real	20	100	17

Chromosome Dataset[49] consists of 22 genetic string sets, each containing 100 individual strings of different lengths. Each string encodes selected parts of a chromosome and is based on an alphabet of 11 different genetic symbols. The Darwin dataset uses 21 lines of Charles Darwin's work "On the Origin of Species", each of which was artificially modified according to common probabilities in optical character recognition applications.[45,50] To generate a set, each one line was duplicated 40 times, while each symbol had a 12% chance to be modified in the process. The modification was a substitution with a different but optical similar symbol in 87%, a deletion in 9% and an insertion of a new symbol in 4% of the cases. Since these lines are written in the English language, 52 symbols are possible with 26 lower and 26 upper case letters. The MSNBC.com anonymous web dataset is a symbolic time series consisting of consecutive page views by users on msnbc.com and msn.com for one day. Each time series is represented by an array of integers, each integer representing a visit to a page of a specific category like news, weather, business and 14 others. The dataset consists of 989818 entries of varying length, from which we randomly selected 20 subsets with 100 entries between 30 and 50 visited pages.

For all datasets, we used the Levenshtein edit distance with cost 1 for deletion, insertion and substitution. The average results of all datasets using five median algorithms are shown in Figure 3. These methods are the greedy algorithm (Section 5.2.1), prototype embedding (Section 5.2.3) and distance-preserving embedding (DPE, Section 5.2.3), evolutionary weighted mean (EWM, Section 5.2.2) and set median (Section 4). Since neither of these methods produces an exact result, the minimal possible $E_S(\bar{p})$ is unknown.

In the case of prototype embedding, DPE and EWM, we did not use parameters specific for these datasets, but parameters that performed well in a range of applications instead. As weighted mean function we used the modified Levenshtein distance described in Section 5.2.2

As can be seen in Figure 3, aside from the MSNBC dataset the greedy algorithm performs significantly worse than all other methods. This can be

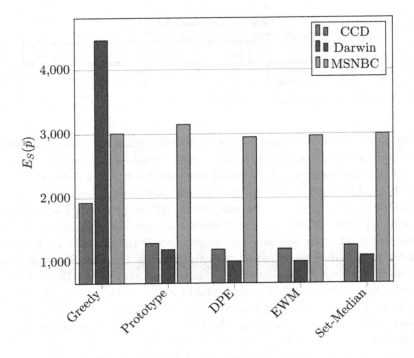

Fig. 3. Experimental results on three datasets using five approximative algorithms. A lower result is better.

explained by the simple nature of the algorithm. By only selecting the next best symbol, it is easy to arrive at a poor local minimum. For example, if the set consists only of the string "AB", then the generalized median is also "AB". Selecting both "A" and "B" as initial symbol of the greedy algorithm result in a distance of 1 (assuming cost 1 for all edit operations). If "B" is selected, then the algorithm stops since the first "A" is never added afterwards and no improvement can be made by adding more symbols at the end. This could also explain the much worse performance in the case of the Darwin dataset. Since there are much more different symbols in this set, the likelihood to select a suboptimal one is much higher. The greedy algorithm performs well in the MSNBC dataset since the first category is "frontpage" which is visited relatively often and is the first visited page of most users. In our case, this is also the first category that is tested as an addition to the solution of the greedy algorithm and therefore causes problems like the ones above not nearly as often as in the other datasets.

The results of prototype embedding are generally better by a large margin, but often slightly worse than the set median which is much easier to calculate. Distance-preserving embedding methods improve this result and are on average better than the set median. This can be attributed to the more accurate embedding, which improves the median computation in vector space and therefore the reconstructed median string.

The evolutionary weighted mean method shows results only slightly worse than distance-preserving embedding, each of them being the best method in several string sets of all datasets.

The set median results demonstrate why it is often used as a good approximation of the generalized median. Even though it is the easiest and fastest of the shown methods, its results are close behind the results of DPE and EWM in the tested datasets.

7. Discussions and Conclusion

This chapter deals with consensus learning for sequence data, in particular strings. Several procedures for computing median strings were briefly described. Experimental results were reported to demonstrate the median concept and to compare some of the discussed algorithms.

The majority of the algorithms described in this chapter are based on the Levenshtein edit distance. The algorithms' applicability to an arbitrary string distance function is summarized in Table 2. Note that an extension to an arbitrary string distance function usually means a computational complexity different from that for the Levenshtein edit distance.

In the definition of median string, all the input strings have a uniform weight of one. If necessary, this basic definition can be easily extended to

Table 2.   Characteristics of median computation algorithms

Algorithm	Distance function (original paper)	Extension to Arbitrary Distance	Handling Weighted Median	Handling Closest String
Exact algorithm and its variants[22,35–37]	Levenshtein	No	Yes	No (yes[36])
Greedy algorithms[38,39]	Levenshtein	Yes	Yes	Yes
Evolutionary weighted mean[40]	Arbitrary distance	n/A	Yes	Yes
Distance-preserving embedding[42,45]	Arbitrary distance	n/A	Yes	Yes[51]
Perturbation-based iterative refinement[21,46]	Arbitrary distance	n/A	Yes	Yes
Dynamic algorithm[48]	Levenshtein	No	Yes	No

weighted median string to model the situation where each string has an individual importance, confidence, etc. Given the weights $w_q, q \in S$, the weighted generalized median string is simply

$$\bar{p} = \arg\min_{p \in U} \sum_{q \in S} w_q \cdot d(p, q).$$

All the computational procedures discussed before can be modified to handle this extension in a straightforward manner.

The generalized median string represents one way of capturing the essential characteristics of a set of strings. There do exist other possibilities. One example is the so-called *closest string*[51] or *center string* defined by:

$$p^* = \arg\min_{p \in U} \max_{q \in S} d(p, q).$$

It is important to note that the term center string is used by Gusfield[4] to denote the set median string. Under the two conditions given in Section 3, it is proven by de la Higuera and Casacuberta[28] that computing the closest string is NP-hard. Another result is given by Frances and Litman[52] where the NP-hardness of the closest string problem is proven for the special case of a binary alphabet (i.e., $\Sigma = \{0, 1\}$) and the Hamming string distance. The ability of the algorithms to compute the closest string is summarized in Table 2.

Another issue of general interest is concerned with cyclic strings. Several methods have been proposed to efficiently compute the Levenshtein distance of cyclic strings.[53–55] It remains an open problem to determine medians of this kind of strings.

References

1. X. Jiang and H. Bunke. Learning by generalized median concept. In ed. P. Wang, *Pattern Recognition and Machine Vision*, pp. 1–16. River Publishers (2010).
2. G. A. Stephen. *String Searching Algorithms*. World Scientific (1994).
3. A. Apostolico and Z. Galil, *Pattern Matching Algorithms*. Oxford University Press (1997).
4. D. Gusfield. *Algorithms on Strings, Trees and Sequences: Computer Science and Computational Biology*. Cambridge University Press (1997).
5. D. Sankoff and J. B. Kruskal, eds., *Time Warps, String Edits, and Macromolecules: The Theory and Practice of Sequence Comparison*. vol. 1, CSLI Publications (2000).
6. M. Crochemore and W. Rytter. *Jewels of Stringology*. World Scientific (2002).
7. M. Crochemore, C. Hancart, and T. Lecroq. *Algorithms on Strings*. Cambridge University Press (2014).

8. S. C. Boulakia, A. Denise, and S. Hamel. Using medians to generate consensus rankings for biological data. In *Proc. of 23rd International Conference on Scientific and Statistical Database Management (SSDBM)*, pp. 73–90 (2011).

9. H. Ding, R. Berezney, and J. Xu. k-prototype learning for 3d rigid structures. In *NIPS*, pp. 2589–2597 (2013).

10. R. I. Hartley, J. Trumpf, Y. Dai, and H. Li, Rotation averaging. *International Journal of Computer Vision*. **103**(3), 267–305 (2013).

11. S. Vega-Pons and J. Ruiz-Shulcloper. A survey of clustering ensemble algorithms, *International Journal of Pattern Recognition and Artificial Intelligence*. **25**(3), 337–372 (2011).

12. X. Jiang, A. Münger, and H. Bunke. On median graphs: properties, algorithms, and applications, *IEEE Transactions on Pattern Analysis and Machine Intelligence*. **23**(10), 1144–1151 (2001).

13. B. Berkels, G. Linkmann, and M. Rumpf. An SL(2) invariant shape median, *Journal of Mathematical Imaging and Vision*. **37**(2), 85–97 (2010).

14. Y. Xie, J. Ho, and B. C. Vemuri. Multiple atlas construction from A heterogeneous brain MR image collection, *IEEE Transactions on Medical Imaging*. **32**(3), 628–635 (2013).

15. T. Lewis, R. Owens, and A. Baddeley. Averaging feature maps, *Pattern Recognition*. **32**(9), 1615–1630 (1999).

16. X. Pennec and N. Ayache. Uniform distribution, distance and expectation problems for geometric features processing, *Journal of Mathematical Imaging and Vision*. **9**(1), 49–67 (1998).

17. A. Guimond, J. Meunier, and J.-P. Thirion. Average brain models: A convergence study, *Computer Vision and Image Understanding*. **77**(2), 192–210 (2000).

18. K. Subramanyan and D. Dean. A procedure to average 3d anatomical structures, *Medical Image Analysis*. **4**(4), 317–334 (2000).

19. A. J. O'Toole, T. Price, T. Vetter, J. Bartlett, and V. Blanz. 3d shape and 2d surface textures of human faces: the role of averages in attractiveness and age, *Image and Vision Computing*. **18**(1), 9–19 (1999).

20. X. Jiang, H. Bunke, and J. Csirik. Median strings: A review. In eds. M. Last, A. Kandel, and H. Bunke, *Data Mining in Time Series Databases*, pp. 173–192. World Scientific (2004).

21. T. Kohonen. Median strings, *Pattern Recognition Letters*. **3**(5), 309–313 (1985).

22. D. Lopresti and J. Zhou. Using consensus sequence voting to correct ocr errors, *Computer Vision and Image Understanding*. **67**(1), 39–47 (1997).

23. C. D. Martinez-Hinarejos, A. Juan, and F. Casacuberta. Improving classification using median string and NN rules. In *Proc. of IX Spanish Symposium on Pattern Recognition and Image Analysis*, pp. 391–395 (2001).

24. R. A. Wagner and M. J. Fischer. The string-to-string correction problem, *Journal of the ACM*. **21**(1), 168–173 (1974).

25. A. Marzal and E. Vidal. Computation of normalized edit distance and applications, *IEEE Transactions on Pattern Analysis and Machine Intelligence*. **15**(9), 926–932 (1993).

26. W. E. Winkler. String comparator metrics and enhanced decision rules in the fellegi-sunter model of record linkage. In *Proceedings of the Section on Survey Research Methods, American Statistical Association*, pp. 354–359 (1990).

27. A. L. Fred and J. M. Leitao. A comparative study of string dissimilarity measures in structural clustering. In *International Conference on Advances in Pattern Recognition*, pp. 385–394 (1999).

28. C. de la Higuera and F. Casacuberta. Topology of strings: Median string is NP-complete, *Theoretical Computer Science*. **230**(1), 39–48 (2000).

29. J. S. Sim and K. Park. The consensus string problem for a metric is np-complete, *Journal of Discrete Algorithms*. **1**(1), 111–117 (2003).

30. F. Nicolas and E. Rivals. Hardness results for the center and median string problems under the weighted and unweighted edit distances, *Journal of Discrete Algorithms*. **3**, 390–415 (2005).

31. L. Wang and T. Jiang. On the complexity of multiple sequence alignment, *Journal of Computational Biology*. **1**(4), 337–348 (1994).

32. A. Juan and E. Vidal. Fast median search in metric spaces. In *Proc. IAPR Workshop on Structural, Syntactic, and Statistical Pattern Recognition*, pp. 905–912 (1998).

33. L. Micó and J. Oncina. An approximate median search algorithm in non-metric spaces, *Pattern Recognition Letters*. **22**(10), 1145–1151 (2001).

34. R. Fagin and L. Stockmeyer. Relaxing the triangle inequality in pattern matching, *International Journal of Computer Vision*. **30**(3), 219–231 (1998).

35. J. B. Kruskal. An overview of sequence comparison: Time warps, string edits, and macromolecules, *SIAM Review*. **25**(2), 201–237 (1983).

36. M. Hayashida and H. Koyano. Integer linear programming approach to median and center strings for a probability distribution on a set of strings, *Proceedings of the 9th International Joint Conference on Biomedial Engineering Systems and Technologies (BIOSTEC 2016)*. **3**, 35–41 (2016).

37. U.-V. Marti and H. Bunke. Use of positional information in sequence alignment for multiple classifier combination. In *Second International Workshop on Multiple Classifier Systems*, pp. 388–398 (2001).

38. F. Casacuberta and M. de Antonio. A greedy algorithm for computing approximate median strings. In *Proc. of National Symposium on Pattern Recognition and Image Analysis*, pp. 193–198 (1997).

39. F. Kruzslicz. Improved greedy algorithm for computing approximate median strings, *Acta Cybernetica*. **14**(2), 331–340 (1999).

40. L. Franek and X. Jiang. Evolutionary weighted mean based framework for generalized median computation with application to strings. In *Proc. IAPR Workshop on Structural, Syntactic, and Statistical Pattern Recognition*, pp. 70–78 (2012).

41. H. Bunke, X. Jiang, K. Abegglen, and A. Kandel. On the weighted mean of a pair of strings, *Pattern Analysis and Applications*. **5**(1), 23–30 (2002).

42. M. Ferrer, E. Valveny, F. Serratosa, K. Riesen, and H. Bunke. Generalized median graph computation by means of graph embedding in vector spaces, *Pattern Recognition*. **43**(4), 1642–1655 (2010).

43. E. Weiszfeld and F. Plastria. On the point for which the sum of the distances to n given points is minimum, *Annals of Operations Research.* **167**(1), 7–41 (2009).

44. A. Nienkötter and X. Jiang. Improved prototype embedding based generalized median computation by means of refined reconstruction methods. In *Proc. IAPR Workshop on Structural, Syntactic, and Statistical Pattern Recognition*, pp. 107–117 (2016).

45. A. Nienkötter and X. Jiang. Distance-preserving vector space embedding for consensus learning, *Submitted for publication* (2017).

46. C. D. Martinez-Hinarejos, A. Juan, and F. Casacuberta. Use of median string for classification. In *15th International Conference on Pattern Recognition*, vol. 2, pp. 903–906 (2000).

47. J. Abreu and J. R. Rico-Juan. A new iterative algorithm for computing a quality approximate median of strings based on edit operations, *Pattern Recognition Letters.* **36**, 74–80 (2014).

48. X. Jiang, K. Abegglen, H. Bunke, and J. Csirik. Dynamic computation of generalised median strings, *Pattern Analysis and Applications.* **6**(3), 185–193 (2003).

49. C. Lundsteen, J. Phillip, and E. Granum. Quantitative analysis of 6985 digitized trypsin G-banded human metaphase chromosomes, *Clinical Genetics.* **18**, 355–370 (1980).

50. X. Jiang, J. Wentker, and M. Ferrer. Generalized median string computation by means of string embedding in vector spaces, *Pattern Recognition Letters.* **33**(7), 842–852 (2012).

51. A. Nienkötter and X. Jiang. Distance-preserving vector space embedding for the closest string problem, *Proceedings of the 23rd International Conference on Pattern Recognition* (2016).

52. M. Frances and A. Litman. On covering problems of codes, *Theory of Computing Systems.* **30**(2), 113–119 (2007).

53. J. Gregor and M. G. Thomason. Dynamic programming alignment of sequences representing cyclic patterns, *IEEE Transactions on Pattern Analysis and Machine Intelligence.* **15**(2), 129–135 (1993).

54. J. Gregor and M. G. Thomason, Efficient dynamic programming alignment of cyclic strings by shift elimination, *Pattern Recognition.* **29**(7), 1179–1185 (1996).

55. A. Marzal and S. Barrachina. Speeding up the computation of the edit distance for cyclic strings. In *15th International Conference on Pattern Recognition*, vol. 2, pp. 891–894 (2000).

Chapter 5

Clustering-Based Classification of Document Streams with Active Learning

Mark Last[*], Maxim Stoliar[†] and Menahem Friedman[‡]

Department of Information Systems Engineering
Ben-Gurion University of the Negev Beer-Sheva 84105, Israel
[*] mlast@bgu.ac.il
[†] max.stoliar@gmail.com
[‡] mlfrid@netvision.net.il

Automated categorization of textual information is becoming an increasingly important task in the digital world. However, most classification algorithms build upon manual labeling of text documents, which is a time-consuming and costly process. In this paper, we present a novel methodology for clustering-based classification of stationary document streams using active learning. The proposed active learning clustering-based classification algorithm (ACCA) obtains a continuous stream of unlabeled documents. The arriving documents are clustered incrementally so that each incoming document is inserted into an existing cluster or used to start a new cluster of its own. The number of possible clusters is unlimited. From time to time, an expert is called to label several clusters for the classification mechanism. With arrival of more documents, the expert can be called less frequently, since most of the incoming documents will eventually belong to existing labeled clusters. Our algorithm is aimed at finding the fastest way of reaching the point where most arriving documents can be classified automatically without the experts assistance. The evaluation experiments on two benchmark corpora show that active learning and clustering can increase the percentage of automatically and accurately categorized documents over time.

1. Introduction

Text categorization, or classification, is a task where texts are assigned to one or several of a set of predefined categories based on their content.[1] If the texts are newspaper articles, typical categories might be, for example, economics, politics, sports, and so on. Text classification applications include automatic email categorization, spam filtering,[2] and web-page classification.[3] These applications are becoming increasingly important in todays information-oriented society.

While many algorithms have been developed in recent years to cope with text classification, a key difficulty is that they require many labeled examples to produce a good classifier that can classify text documents with high accuracy. The labeling in text classification is typically done manually by reading documents or web pages, which is a time-consuming task. Unfortunately, we cannot eliminate the document labeling process, since without it a supervised machine learning algorithm will not be able to build an accurate classifier representing the user interests.

The task addressed in this paper is classification of a stream of incoming documents where there are no labeled documents at the starting point. Classification is often posed as supervised learning, where a set of labeled data is used to train a classifier that can be applied to label future examples. According to Ref. 4, in batch classification algorithms the same time-consuming and computationally expensive training process has to be run again in order to adjust the classifier when receiving new data. Moreover, labeling documents is costly and it would be too expensive to employ experts all the time on labeling every new document found on the web.

In order to reduce the computational effort and the amount of labeled documents, our methodology uses incremental clustering. Considering a continuous and stationary document stream, we either assign each arriving document to an existing cluster or start a new cluster. The number of possible clusters is unlimited. At some stage, an expert is asked to label a selected number of clusters. Cluster labeling by the expert is based on representative documents from that cluster. All documents in each labeled cluster are assigned the same label.

In this work, we present an active learning algorithm (ACCA) for clustering-based classification of document streams. Our method requires no initial training set. Unlike other methods that use clustering for text categorization and active learning (such as Refs. 4 and 5), our method does not limit the amount of possible clusters and allows the active learner to label clusters rather than just single documents. We show that although at the starting point there are no labeled documents, it is possible to improve classification accuracy over time by using active learning and to reduce the amount of documents that need to be labeled. Consequently, we will submit fewer queries to the experts for labeling documents that belong to new, unlabeled clusters.

The rest of this chapter is organized as follows. Section 2 describes the related work on active learning, incremental clustering, and clustering-based text categorization. Section 3 presents the active learning clustering-based classification (ACCA) algorithm. Section 4 presents the experimental settings used for the evaluation of the proposed method and discusses the results of the evaluation experiments. Section 5 summarizes this chapter and outlines the directions for future research.

2. Related Work

This section covers the research in several domains, which are relevant to the proposed method. Sub-section 2.1 describes several approaches to incremental clustering, including fuzzy-based clustering. Sub-section 2.2 presents active learning and discusses various active learning techniques. In sub-section 2.3, we cover existing clustering-based classification methods with and without active learning.

2.1. *Incremental Clustering*

A method for clustering-based categorization of a continuous document stream should be able to use its accumulated knowledge at any stage during the learning process. This implies that the learned patterns evolve with every new instance and there is no need of repeatedly processing previous instances. This sort of clustering is referred to as an *incremental clustering*.[6] Incremental clustering involves several challenges. The number of arriving documents at the early stages of a document stream is small making it difficult to obtain a high degree of clustering quality. As additional documents arrive, it might become necessary to re-assign some previously arrived documents to new clusters. In other words, document streams with a different arrival order may result in different clustering results. Due to these and other problems, there is still much work to be done before an incremental clustering method can be regarded as accurate.[7]

According to Ref. 8, an important advantage of incremental clustering algorithms is that it is not necessary to store the entire dataset in the computer memory. Consequently, the space requirements of incremental algorithms are very small. In Ref. 8, an example of an incremental algorithm is presented. In the first step of the algorithm, the first document is assigned to the first cluster. In the next steps, when a new item arrives, it is assigned either to one of the existing clusters or to a new cluster. The cluster assignment of a new document is based on the distance between the new document and the existing cluster centroids.

In *fuzzy clustering*, instead of associating an item with a cluster, a membership function relates a document to a pattern. In Ref. 9, a fuzzy-based method for incremental clustering of text documents is presented. With this method, documents are represented as keyphrase vectors, similar to the vector-space model,[10] and the cluster centroid is defined by averaging the vectors already assigned to this cluster. The centroid must include all keyphrases that belong to any of the vectors in the cluster. For each keyphrase, the averaging function takes into account only the documents containing that particular keyphrase rather than all documents in the cluster. Since the method is an incremental clustering algorithm, incoming vectors are processed one at a time. Before a new cluster is created, the similarity to each cluster centroid is computed treating each of its keyphrases separately and assigning them importance degrees with respect to the cluster. The document is assigned to the most similar cluster provided that the distance of the vector to the associated cluster centroid does not exceed a given threshold. If it exceeds the threshold, a new cluster is created.

The important feature of this method is that the final number of clusters is determined by the algorithm rather than being limited by the user. The only requirement is that each cluster will include similar vectors; vectors that belong to separate clusters will be radically different. In Ref. 11, the methods presented in Ref. 9 are revised and several crisp and fuzzy methods based on the cosine similarity principle for clustering without limiting the final number of clusters are presented. Removing the restriction on the total number of clusters moderately increases computation costs but it improves the methods performance in classifying incoming vectors as normal or abnormal, based on their similarity to existing clusters.

2.2. *Active Learning*

A general principle in machine learning is that the more training data a learner has, the more accurate it should be. In practice, machine learning algorithms are trained with very large amounts of training data due to the fact that not all examples are equally informative. Some possess little or no information value while others are extremely informative. In active learning, the learner queries a large data pool for data points that are expected to be the most informative. Active learners are useful when labeling a data point is expensive. With active learning, a machine learning algorithm can achieve higher accuracy with fewer labelled training instances. An active learner can present queries to an expert (a human annotator), a query being a case from the input domain for which the learner does not know the real label. These queries are the heart of the active learning framework and allow the learner to control the training data it uses.

A *stopping criterion* is a potentially important element of interactive learning algorithms and it is used to decide when to stop the active learning process. In most cases, a simple stopping criterion allows the expert to provide a specified number of labels, which is called the *labeling budget*. In other approaches, referred to as holdout accuracy approaches, the algorithm stops when the performance of the classifier reaches a point where the cost of acquiring new training data is greater than the cost of the errors made by the current model. The stopping criteria that use the intrinsic characteristics of the classifiers are preferable since they do not require a testing set.[12]

In *pool-based active learning*, the learner is provided with a set of independent and identically-distributed unlabeled instances. At each step, the active learner chooses an unlabeled instance to request the label from the expert by means of a querying function. In the case of text categorization problems, the queries presented to the expert are documents from the domain. Since these are comprehensible to the expert, a correct label can be assigned.[13] In the literature, there exist several methods for choosing unlabeled instances for the expert to label. One of those methods is uncertainty sampling,[13] which uses a selective sampling criterion. It is accomplished by selecting an instance based on a confidence score in the classification of the instance. The instances having the lowest confidence scores are supposed to be the most beneficial for labeling.

The *query by committee* (QBC) algorithm is an approach to version space reduction that involves maintaining a committee of models, which are all trained on the labeled set, but represent competing hypotheses. During learning, whenever an unlabeled instance is available, the algorithm selects two random hypotheses from the committee and only queries for the label of the new instance if the two hypotheses disagree.[14] This is a *stream-based* selection algorithm where the learner is given access to a stream of unlabeled examples taken randomly from the input space according to some unknown distribution. With time, the prediction capabilities of the learner will improve and it will discard the majority of the examples drawn from the stream. In the initial stage, the learner queries the expert extensively, but this effort is reduced over time.

Reference 15 presents an active learning framework for drifting (non-stationary) data streams, which builds a new classifier every time it detects a decrease in the current classifier accuracy. The framework assumes that no historical data can be stored in memory implying that the expert should always be available for labeling some of the incoming instances immediately upon their arrival. The framework expresses the labeling budget as a fraction of all incoming data.

Reference 16 presents a cloud-based scientific workflow platform Clowd-Flows for online dynamic adaptive sentiment analysis of microblogging posts. The ClowdFlows platform uses the stream–based active learning approach, where examples are constantly arriving from a data stream and the learning algorithm has to decide in real time whether to select an arriving example for labeling or not. In a practical experiment, the arriving tweets are split into batches of fixed size (100) and a constant portion of each batch (10 tweets) is selected for manual labeling. The tweets selected for labeling include 3 most uncertain tweets along with 7 random tweets.

2.3. *Clustering-Based Classification*

In most text categorization tasks, labeled examples (e.g., documents or tweets) are costly to obtain, whereas unlabeled examples are much cheaper to collect. The document–labeling requirement is a key difficulty in text categorization algorithms, since without many labeled examples it is hard to produce a good classifier that can classify text documents with high accuracy. As recent studies indicate, unlabeled data can contribute to the learning process. That is, the *semi-supervised learning* approach, which uses both labeled and unlabeled data for text categorization is better than supervised learning based on a small set of labeled data alone.

References 4 and 17 propose a text classification algorithm that combines supervised and unsupervised learning. The reasoning behind this approach is that if some structure exists in the objects, it is possible to take advantage of this information and to find a short description of the data. The difference between this algorithm and others is that given a classification problem, the training and testing examples are both clustered before the classification step. This is a rather time–consuming and computationally expensive process. As a possible extension of their work, Ref. 17 suggests using incremental clustering to handle the arrival of new documents.

In the method proposed by Ref. 18, unsupervised classification is seen as a preprocessing step that is performed only once. Then, depending on the availability of labeled samples, the supervised classification is applied. Since in real-world problems classes are not generally well separated, it is possible to have samples from different classes in one cluster or no sample of a given class in others. To avoid this, the method uses a combination of multiple clustering methods e.g., EM and k-means. The authors show that adding more clusters improves the classification performance since the objects are described in more detail.

Active learning can be used together with clustering to improve the classification accuracy of an incoming stream of documents or emails as demonstrated by Ref. 19 who use a two-class active learning methodology that incorporates active learning and clustering. The algorithm first constructs a classifier from a set of cluster representatives and then propagates the classification decision to other samples via a local noise model. The algorithm of Ref. 19 uses a soft cluster membership technique, which allows a sample to be related to more than one cluster.

The authors of Ref. 2 present an active semi-supervised learning approach, which helps spam filters to better detect spam mail. One of the problems the method is designed to solve is the unwillingness of the users to label a large amount of emails that the spam filter is uncertain of. To solve this difficulty, unlabeled emails are clustered and the label of one email in each cluster, which is assumed to contain only spam or only ham emails, is determined by the user. Such a label is propagated to similar emails in the same cluster meaning that now the user does not have to label many emails. Emails labeled by the user and by label propagation are used to re-train the spam filter. The remaining emails can be clustered again to repeat the whole process until the user is unwilling to label additional emails.

Thus, the current methods for clustering-based text categorization, suffer from the following limitations:

- The active learning methods for clustering-based text categorization are batch methods, which cannot handle labeling of new arriving documents or update document clusters over time.
- In most text-categorization methods that use clustering, the number of clusters is limited, which causes impurity problems with some of the clusters.
- Clustering-based methods that do not limit the number of clusters, such as Ref. 11, do not utilize active learning mechanisms.

3. Methodology

This section presents an active learning algorithm for clustering-based classification of an incoming stream of text documents.

3.1. *Methodology Overview*

The proposed methodology deals with a stationary stream of unlabeled documents. Since our algorithm uses clustering to classify new documents and active learning to significantly reduce the amount of label queries that the clustering-based classifier requires, we call it Active learning Clustering–based Classification Algorithm (ACCA).

Each arriving document is inserted into an existing cluster or starts a new cluster of its own, without limiting the total number of created clusters. Once in a while, an expert is called and asked to label several clusters based on their medoid documents. All documents in a cluster are assigned the label given to its medoid. The same label is also associated with each new document assigned to that cluster. We assume that as more arriving documents belong to already labeled clusters, the amount of expert calls should decrease dramatically.

ACCA uses an incremental clustering approach, as opposed to the clustering-based classification algorithm of Ref. 17, which uses a static clustering methodology. Moreover, the amount of clusters in their algorithm is pre-defined, in contrast to ACCA, which does not limit the number of clusters in advance. The spam detection algorithms presented in Refs. 20 and 2 use active learning like ACCA does. However, these algorithms do not use incremental clustering and limit the number of clusters that can be created. In this paper, we show that removing the restriction on the total number of clusters can improve the classification accuracy of a clustering-based classifier.

To sum up, the unique properties of the proposed ACCA methodology for clustering-based classification of stationary document streams include the following:

- It uses clustering-based active learning to reduce the amount of documents that need to be labeled by an expert.
- It does not require the expert to be always available for immediate labeling of selected incoming documents by occasionally calling the expert for a batch labeling of several unlabeled clusters.
- It removes the restriction on the total number of clusters to handle mul-

tiple topics and subtopics.

- It uses incremental clustering to improve the classification accuracy with each new arriving document.
- It uses an advanced, keyphrase-based representation of text documents.

3.2. *Active Learning Clustering-based Classification Algorithm (ACCA)*

The detailed step-by-step description of the ACCA algorithm is provided below.

Input: The input of the algorithm is a stationary stream of unlabeled textual documents, which belong to a fixed and known set of classes (e.g., 'spam' and 'not-spam' emails). The assumption is that the stream can keep going forever although in our evaluation experiments we were limited with the amount of documents in the available datasets.

Output: Each incoming document either is assigned to one of the known classes (based on the label of its cluster) or is identified as an unknown type of document (if its cluster has not been labeled yet). These unlabeled documents are eventually classified by the algorithm after their respective clusters are labeled by a domain expert.

The algorithm has the following parameters:

- *Similarity threshold* - can take a value between zero and one. When the document similarity to the nearest cluster is below this threshold, it starts a new cluster.
- *Clustering method* - in our experiments, we used either cosine or fuzzy cosine clustering methods. These methods are explained below.
- *Cluster labeling strategy* - we used one of the following strategies for choosing the clusters to be labeled by the expert: random sampling, density calculation, cluster size, and radius calculation. These strategies are explained below.
- *Percentage of unlabeled clusters* chosen for the expert labeling. We used the following values in our experiments: 15%, 50% and 100%.

3.2.1. *Step 1: Document Representation*

We use the GenEx algorithm[21] to represent each document by a list of keyphrases and a vector of their importance weights (scores). In Ref. 21, the concept of keyphrases is defined. A keyphrase may be a single keyword or a phrase (n-gram) of 2-3 consecutive words. A keyphrase list is defined by

Ref. 21 as a short list of phrases (typically 5-15 noun-phrases) that capture the main topics discussed in a given document. Thus, each document may be represented by a vector of k keyphrase weights ($1 \leq k \leq m$) where m is the maximum number of keyphrases in a given document. The score w_{ji} of a keyphrase t_i in a document d_j is calculated by the GenEx algorithm as a function of the keyphrase in-document frequency and the location of the first appearance of each word stem comprising the keyphrase.

3.2.2. *Step 2: Document Clustering*

At the beginning of the process, there are no documents. As we start obtaining documents via a document stream, we apply the document representation model presented in Step 1 to the incoming documents. The documents obtained from the stream are clustered upon their arrival. Since we focus in our work on massive document streams, we may not be aware of all possible topics and subtopics presented by the incoming documents. To avoid information loss that may affect the performance during the classification phase, we do not limit the number of clusters, similar to the approach presented in Ref. 9.

In our evaluation experiments, we use two incremental clustering algorithms: Crisp Cosine Clustering (CCC) and Fuzzy-Based Cosine Clustering (FCC). Both algorithms, which are presented in Ref. 9, process one arriving vector at a time. When the first document arrives, it forms a new cluster. Each cluster is represented by its centroid. Both algorithms are partitioning clustering algorithms, which produce a flat partition of documents into clusters.

The Crisp Cosine Clustering (CCC) algorithm defines the cluster centroid c as a normalized vector of the sum of all vectors already in the cluster C:

$$c = \sum_j w_{ji} \bigg/ \bigg\| \sum_j w_{ji} \bigg\|, d_j \in C \tag{1}$$

where the importance weights w_{ji} are normalized with respect to the Euclidean norm $\| \sum_j w_{ji} \|$ of the centroid. To measure the similarity between an incoming vector $v = (v_1, .., v_m)$ and a centroid $c = (c_1, , c_m)$, as v arrives, the CCC algorithm normalizes the importance weights of v with respect to its Euclidean norm $\|v\|$ and then calculates the inner product similarity by Eq. (2), which considers only keyphrases that appear in both vectors:

$$s = c \cdot v = \sum_{k=1}^{m} (c_k \cdot v_k) \tag{2}$$

The Fuzzy-Based Cosine Clustering (FCC) algorithm assigns to each incoming vector v a grade of membership $\chi(v, c)$, which is a number between 0 and 1, computed as a function of the ratio $\|v\|/\|c\|$ between the Euclidean norm of the document vector and the Euclidean norm of the cluster centroid. The similarity is then defined as:

$$s = \chi(v, c)(c \cdot v)/(\|v\| \cdot \|c\|) \tag{3}$$

The membership function between v and c is defined as the fraction:

$$\chi(v, c) = \begin{cases} \frac{9}{4}\alpha^2(1 - \alpha), & \alpha \le \frac{2}{3} \\ 1, & \alpha > \frac{2}{3} \end{cases} \tag{4}$$

where $\alpha = \|v\|/\|c\|$ is the relative size of v with respect to c. The above membership function is proportional to α as long as α is relatively small (less than a pre–defined threshold). For all values of α above the threshold, the function is constant and equal to one. Based on Ref. 11, the threshold we use in Eq. (4) is 2/3. Consequently, the document-cluster similarity of vectors, which are much smaller in size than the cluster centroid c (less than 2/3 of its norm) will be lower than the "crisp" cosine similarity, which totally ignores the size of the vector v.

Finally, both algorithms (CCC and FCC) assign the vector v to the cluster that produces the maximum similarity (calculated by Eqs. (2) and (3), respectively), provided it is above a pre–defined similarity threshold. If all similarity values are below this threshold, the incoming vector starts a new cluster. Both algorithms do not limit the number of clusters, leading to continuous creation of new clusters with arrival of new documents, which are dissimilar to existing clusters. The new clusters will be small (containing just one document in the beginning) and thus more pure (homogeneous).

3.2.3. *Step 3: Calling the Expert*

The arriving documents are clustered using an incremental clustering algorithm (such as CCC or FCC). In the beginning of the document stream, no cluster has a class label and consequently, all arriving documents are unlabeled as well. After the arrival of x documents, a domain expert is called for the first time. The number x is specified by the user based on the document arrival rate and other constraints. Every time an expert is called, he/she is asked to label a certain percentage p of unlabeled clusters. The percentage p is specified by the user, based mainly on the labeling budget, since assigning a label to each cluster requires reading the content of a document, which is the medoid of that cluster. We assume that only one label can be assigned to each cluster.

The expert is called again after the arrival of another x unlabeled documents, which do not belong to any of previously labeled clusters. Assuming that the document stream is stationary and the document arrival rate is relatively stable, we expect the time intervals between the successive expert calls to increase over time along with a decrease in the actual number of clusters the expert is asked to label upon each call. Thus, if there is a fixed cost associated with each expert call and another fixed cost for each labeled cluster, the total cost of expert services should decrease over time.

3.2.4. *Step 4: Choosing the clusters to label*

Every time the expert is called, we ask him to label y unlabeled clusters, which are then used by the clustering-based classifier. In our experiments, we have evaluated the following strategies for choosing the clusters to label:

- *Random Sampling* - With random sampling, the clusters brought to the expert are chosen randomly from the set of still unlabeled clusters. The random sampling method is used as a baseline for comparison to all other methods.
- *Cluster Density* - Cluster density is defined as an average similarity of each document to all other documents in a cluster. Density is calculated by:

$$density = \frac{\sum_{i=1}^{n} \sum_{j=1}^{n} s(x_i, x_j)}{n} \qquad (5)$$

The n parameter in Eq. (5) is the number of documents in a given cluster and $s(x_i, x_j)$ represents similarity between documents x_i and x_j. In our evaluation experiments, we test if preferring more dense clusters for the expert labeling may improve the performance of a clustering-based classifier.
- *Cluster Size* With this strategy, we bring to the expert the medoids of the largest clusters that the expert has not labeled yet. By choosing this strategy, we assume that the clusters already having more documents than others will continue to obtain more documents from the incoming stream and thus should be preferred for labeling.
- *Cluster Radius* - Cluster radius, similar to the cluster density, is defined as an average distance of the cluster documents to the cluster medoid.

Radius is calculated the following way:

$$radius = \frac{\sum_{i=1}^{n} d(x_i, m)}{n} \tag{6}$$

The n parameter in Eq. (6) is the number of documents in a given cluster. In our evaluation experiments, we test if preferring clusters with a smaller radius may improve the performance of a clustering-based classifier.

3.2.5. *Step 5: Cluster Labeling*

For each of y clusters that the expert is asked to label, we calculate the cluster medoid. The medoid is defined as the most centrally located item in a cluster, i.e., this is the document, which has the minimal average distance to all other documents in the cluster. When the expert receives a medoid and labels it, we assign the same label to all documents in the cluster. When a new document is assigned to a labeled cluster, it is labeled as having the class of the cluster. Thus, the expert provides us with knowledge for the clustering-based classification mechanism.

3.2.6. *Step 6: Stopping Criteria*

The purpose of active learning is to improve the accuracy of the learner while remaining sensitive to data labeling costs. It is therefore reasonable to stop the active learning process if it does not provide a significant improvement in the classification performance anymore. In our evaluation experiments, we seek to determine the fastest way of reaching the point where the majority of arriving documents can be classified without an expert, since they are assigned to a labeled cluster, and the difference in classification performance between successive expert calls is minimal. After that point, additional expert calls will not be justified and the algorithm can continue classifying incoming documents on its own, under the assumption that the arriving data is generated by a stationary process.

4. Evaluation

We have evaluated the proposed method on two document corpora from two different domains. The goal was to find the best algorithm settings that will provide the fastest way of reaching the point where nearly all arriving documents are labeled without the expert's assistance. We proceed below with describing in detail the corpora, the data preprocessing operations, and the experimental setup.

4.1. *Datasets*

The first document corpus, the TREC07p email corpus, was used in Ref. 2. It is available at http://plg.uwaterloo.ca/~gvcormac/treccorpus07/. This corpus contains all emails delivered to a particular server between 08/04/2007 and 06/06/2007 and it includes desired emails i.e., ham emails, and spam emails. Out of the 75, 419 mails in the corpus, 25, 220 are ham and 50, 199 are spam.

The second corpus used in this work consists of a set of 582 terrorist documents and 21,528 normal documents. The terrorist documents were downloaded from various militant Jihadi websites in English, while the normal documents were collected by passive and anonymous eavesdropping on a small network of university computers used by students from a university department. The documents are from different periods in time and deal with various topics. This corpus was previously used in Ref. 3.

4.2. *Preprocessing*

We cleaned the documents before running the experiments. In the TREC07p corpus, MIME tags were removed and the documents were left only with data relevant to their classification. In the course of this process, we discovered that 4,229 of the documents were either empty or invalid. These documents were removed and were not used in the experiments. What remained was a corpus composed of 71,190 email documents of which 25,113 were ham emails and 46,077 spam emails.

To create a vector representation of each document, we used the Extractor tool which is based on the GenEx algorithm.[21] The GenEx algorithm selects the most important keyphrases in a document and represents each document as a vector of keyphrase weights. The algorithm determines a list of keyphrases that represent the main content of a given document under two conditions. The first condition is a vector-size limitation that is given as an input from the user. In this case, the algorithm chooses the keyphrases that are most representative of each document (have the highest importance weights). The second condition removes from the keyphrase list the phrases that do not provide information about the document content such as conjunctions and other stopwords. In our experiments, we limited the vector size of each document to the maximum of 20 keyphrases. Since different documents in the same corpus may be represented by completely different keyphrase vectors, the total size of the corpus vocabulary is bounded by $20N$, where N is the number of corpus documents.

4.3. *Experimental Setup*

In our experiments, we used the following parameters to determine the best settings for reaching a point where most incoming documents are classified correctly by the ACCA algorithm as quickly as possible.

Similarity threshold. The similarity threshold is used to determine whether the similarity value calculated by formula Eq. (2) is high enough for a document to be added to the nearest cluster or it should start a new cluster. This threshold affects the amount and the content of the clusters labeled and used by the ACCA algorithm. In our experiments, we used the similarity thresholds of 0.1, 0.15, 0.2 and 0.3. In the preliminary runs of the algorithm we found that a threshold higher than 0.3 produced a very large amount of clusters whereas a threshold lower than 0.1 produced too few clusters.

Clustering algorithm. The clustering algorithm used by ACCA is of a key importance. It affects the way the clusters are created, the amount of created clusters, the assignment of documents to clusters, and finally the cluster labeling process performed by the expert. In our experiments, we used the following two clustering algorithms (see sub-section 3.2.2):

- Crisp Cosine Clustering.[22]
- Fuzzy-based Cosine Clustering.[9]

These clustering algorithms were chosen since they are incremental and they do not limit in advance the amount of created clusters. In addition, these and similar algorithms have demonstrated a reasonable performance for detection of anomalous web documents in our previous work.[9,11,22]

Cluster Selection Strategy. During the active learning phase of the ACCA algorithm, the expert obtains a certain amount of clusters to label. Each cluster is represented by one document, which is the medoid of that cluster. The clusters to label are chosen using several strategies. In our experiments, we use the following selection strategies, which were fully discussed in sub-section 3.2.2 above: random sampling, cluster density, cluster size, and cluster radius.

Cluster Labeling Percentage. Every time the expert is called, he is asked to label some percentage of unlabeled clusters. In our experiments, we tested the values of 15%, 50% and 100% of unlabeled clusters that were selected for labeling by the expert.

As explained above, the ACCA algorithm has four parameters. Using combinations of those parameters, we composed a series of experiments.

The following settings were evaluated:

- Four values of the similarity threshold $(0.1, 0.15, 0.2, 0.3)$
- Two clustering algorithms (crisp cosine and fuzzy cosine)
- Four clustering strategies (random sampling, density calculation, cluster size, radius calculation).
- Three values of cluster labeling percentage $(15\%, 50\%, 100\%)$.

Thus, we have conducted 96 experiments per dataset representing the Cartesian product of these settings $(4 \cdot 2 \cdot 4 \cdot 3 = 96)$ and a total of 192 experiments for both datasets.

4.4. *Performance Metrics*

We have used the following metrics to measure the quality of the algorithm results and to find the best combination of parameter settings.

Identification Rate. We refer to identified documents as documents that at the end of the experiment were assigned to one of the labeled clusters, regardless of what their real class was. The identification rate of each experiment was calculated using the following formula:

$$Identification\_rate = \frac{Amount\_of\_identified\_documents}{Total\_amount\_of\_documents} \quad (7)$$

False Positive Error Rate. We refer to false positive documents as ham/non-terror documents that were classified falsely as spam/terror documents. The False Positive Error Rate of each experiment was calculated using the following formula:

$$FalsePositiveErrorRate = \frac{Amount\_of\_false\_positive\_documents}{Amount\_of\_identified\_documents} \quad (8)$$

False Negative Error Rate. We refer to false negative documents as spam/terror documents that were classified falsely as ham/non-terror documents. The False Negative Error Rate of each experiment was calculated using the following formula:

$$FalseNegativeErrorRate = \frac{Amount\_of\_false\_negative\_documents}{Amount\_of\_identified\_documents} \quad (9)$$

Expert Labeling Cost. We define C as the labeling cost of a single expert call in the following way:

$$C = a + y \cdot c \quad (10)$$

The total cost of one expert visit is represented by C, whereas a is the fixed cost of the expert's call and c is the cost of labeling a single document.

We define y as the number of documents the expert labeled during a single call. In this work, we take a as equal to 100 and c as equal to 1, which simply means that the fixed cost of the expert's call is equal to the cost of labeling 100 documents.

4.5. *Analysis of Results*

4.5.1. *Clustering algorithm effect*

The clustering algorithm used by ACCA affects the amount of created clusters, the content of each cluster, the labeling queries submitted to the expert, and finally the clustering-based classification decisions of the algorithm. Table 1 and Table 2 show the effect of clustering algorithms on the obtained results for the terror and the email datasets, respectively.

Table 1.   Evaluation of clustering algorithms in the terror dataset

Algorithm		Min	Max	Mean	Std. Deviation
Crisp	Document Identification rate (%)	77.96	99.65	93.97	5.48
Cosine	False Positive Error Rate (%)	0.56	1.69	1.00	0.395
	False Negative Error Rate (%)	0	0.2	0.003	0.009
	Expert labeling cost	1044	3224	1797	654
Fuzzy	Document Identification rate (%)	71.64	99.38	93.51	7.07
Cosine	False Positive Error Rate (%)	0.411	0.74	0.58	0.13
	False Negative Error Rate (%)	0	0.43	0.00	0.000
	Expert labeling cost	2614	5562	3787	899

Table 2.   Evaluation of clustering algorithms in the email dataset

Algorithm		Min	Max	Mean	Std. Deviation
Crisp	Document Identification rate (%)	89.77	99.49	97.42	2.7
Cosine	False Positive Error Rate (%)	0.61	2.24	1.40	0.65
	False Negative Error Rate (%)	1.18	3.61	2.31	0.63
	Expert labeling cost	1569	8908	4250	2448
Fuzzy	Document Identification rate (%)	90.89	99.98	97.96	2.42
Cosine	False Positive Error Rate (%)	0.43	1.21	0.69	0.221
	False Negative Error Rate (%)	1.61	4.93	3.12	0.844
	Expert labeling cost	6509	17595	11007	3813

It is evident from both tables that the cost of expert labeling with the fuzzy cosine is several times higher than the cost of expert labeling with the crisp cosine. This is because the fuzzy cosine algorithm tends to create more clusters and thus needs more clusters to be labeled by the expert. However, the False Positive Error Rate with the fuzzy cosine algorithm is nearly two times lower than with the crisp cosine algorithm. T-tests have shown that the difference in the False Positive Error Rate is statistically significant in both datasets. On the other hand, in the email dataset, the False Negative Error Rate with the crisp cosine clustering is significantly lower than with the fuzzy cosine algorithm. The document identification rates are quite high in both datasets disregarding the clustering algorithm. The mean Kappa Statistic[23] values for the terror dataset are 0.834 and 0.898 with the Crisp Cosine and the Fuzzy Cosine algorithms, respectively. In the email dataset, which is less imbalanced, the mean Kappa Statistic values are higher: 0.919 (CCC) and 0.918 (FCC).

4.5.2. *Cluster Selection Strategy Effect*

On each call, the expert receives a certain amount of clusters to label. Those clusters can be selected using several strategies. Table 3 and Table 4 show the effect of cluster selection strategies on the obtained results in the terror and the email datasets, respectively.

Table 3. Evaluation of cluster selection strategies in the terror dataset

Strategy		Min.	Max.	Mean	Std. Deviation
Random	Document Identification rate (%)	71.63	99.64	88.62	10.27
	False Positive Error Rate (%)	0.41	1.69	0.88	0.44
	False Negative Error Rate (%)	0	0	0	0
	Expert labeling cost	1115	5562	2943.75	1210.82
Density	Document Identification rate (%)	89.81	99.64	95.15	3.01
	False Positive Error Rate (%)	0.43	1.4	0.78	0.34
	False Negative Error Rate (%)	0	0.04	0.01	0.01
	Expert labeling cost	1044	5562	2718.46	1306.00
Radius	Document Identification rate (%)	90.13	99.68	95.560	2.72
	False Positive Error Rate (%)	0.43	1.43	0.79	0.35
	False Negative Error Rate (%)	0	0.03	0.004	0.01
	Expert labeling cost	1087	5562	2765.88	1283.85
Size	Document Identification rate (%)	90.13	99.65	95.57	2.72
	False Positive Error Rate (%)	0.43	1.43	0.79	0.35
	False Negative Error Rate (%)	0	0.03	0.004	0.01
	Expert labeling cost	1048	5562	2741.75	1343.05

Table 4. Evaluation of cluster selection strategies in the email dataset

Strategy		Min.	Max.	Mean	Std. Deviation
Random	Document Identification rate (%)	89.70	99.98	96.11	4.1
	False Positive Error Rate (%)	0.43	2.24	1.08	0.6
	False Negative Error Rate (%)	1.18	4.93	2.71	1.22
	Expert labeling cost	2080	17595	8221	4691
Density	Document Identification rate (%)	94.54	99.98	98.13	1.66
	False Positive Error Rate (%)	0.44	2.09	1.03	0.61
	False Negative Error Rate (%)	1.71	4.93	2.78	1.18
	Expert labeling cost	1569	17283	7349	4681
Radius	Document Identification rate (%)	95.07	99.98	98.24	1.56
	False Positive Error Rate (%)	0.44	2.23	1.05	0.67
	False Negative Error Rate (%)	1.52	4.93	2.63	1.18
	Expert labeling cost	1602	17283	7464	4760
Size	Document Identification rate (%)	95.43	99.98	98.29	1.47
	False Positive Error Rate (%)	0.44	2.09	1.02	0.62
	False Negative Error Rate (%)	1.66	4.93	2.74	1.13
	Expert labeling cost	1571	17283	7478	4745

In both datasets, we have not found significant differences between various cluster selection strategies using ANOVA, although the false positive \negative rates are higher with the random selection strategy. This makes the random strategy inferior to all non-random strategies evaluated by us.

4.5.3. *Cluster labeling percentage effect*

Every time the expert is called, he is asked to label a certain amount of unlabeled clusters. This amount is defined as a percentage of currently unlabeled clusters. In our experiments, we evaluated the values of 15%, 50%, and 100% of unlabeled clusters. The results are shown in Tables 5 and 6.

As expected, the identification rate increases as a larger percentage of clusters is selected from the set of unlabeled clusters. Not surprisingly, the increase in the identification rate is accompanied by an increase in the expert labeling cost. The false positive \false negative percentage grows as more clusters are labeled though its growth is statistically insignificant. Running ANOVA on the results has shown that the difference between choosing 15%, 50%, and 100% of unlabeled clusters is insignificant in all parameters, except the lower identification rate and the higher labeling cost with the 15% labeling. This means that we can choose 50% of unlabeled

Table 5.   Evaluation of cluster labeling percentages in the terror dataset

Cluster ratio		Min	Max	Mean	Std. Deviation
15%	Document Identification rate (%)	71.64	94.62	88.29	8.01
	False Positive Error Rate (%)	0.43	1.69	0.76	0.37
	False Negative Error Rate (%)	0	0.04	0.01	0.01
	Expert labeling cost	1044	4742	2593	1103
50%	Document Identification rate (%)	91.18	97.9	94.97	1.891
	False Positive Error Rate (%)	0.41	1.46	0.8	0.36
	False Negative Error Rate (%)	0	0	0	0
	Expert labeling cost	1087	5371	2819	1320
100%	Document Identification rate (%)	95.98	99.65	97.97	1.63
	False Positive Error Rate (%)	0.46	1.48	0.82	0.37
	False Negative Error Rate (%)	0	0	0	0
	Expert labeling cost	1115	5562	2966	1381

Table 6.   Evaluation of cluster labeling percentages in the email dataset

Cluster ratio		Min	Max	Mean	Std. Deviation
15%	Document Identification rate (%)	89.77	97.58	94.92	2.69
	False Positive Error Rate (%)	0.43	2.24	1.1	0.63
	False Negative Error Rate (%)	1.18	3.91	2.38	0.96
	Expert labeling cost	1569	17595	7310	4624
50%	Document Identification rate (%)	97.72	99.52	98.6	0.5
	False Positive Error Rate (%)	0.44	2.01	0.99	0.57
	False Negative Error Rate (%)	1.67	4.87	2.82	1.16
	Expert labeling cost	1602	17410	7809	4742
100%	Document Identification rate (%)	99.05	99.98	99.56	0.35
	False Positive Error Rate (%)	0.44	2.09	1.05	0.64
	False Negative Error Rate (%)	1.1	4.93	2.94	1.27
	Expert labeling cost	2080	17283	7766	4737

clusters and still obtain classification performance comparable to 100%. This may be explained by the fact that when labeling 50% of documents the expert skips small clusters, which have a minimal effect on the overall clustering-based classification accuracy.

4.5.4. *Similarity Threshold Effect*

The similarity threshold is used to determine whether an incoming document should be assigned to an existing cluster or start a new cluster. In Tables 7 and 8, we show the effect of the similarity threshold on the results in the terror and the email datasets, respectively.

Table 7.   The similarity threshold effect in the terror dataset

Similarity		Min	Max	Mean	Std. Deviation
0.1	Document Identification rate (%)	74	99.15	94.1	6.63
	False Positive Error Rate (%)	0.75	1.47	1.21	0.23
	False Negative Error Rate (%)	0	0.13	0.03	0.05
	Expert labeling cost	1044	2915	1991.25	831.45
0.15	Document Identification rate (%)	72.25	99.94	94.53	6.45
	False Positive Error Rate (%)	0.74	1.57	1.16	0.2
	False Negative Error Rate (%)	0	0.14	0.03	0.04
	Expert labeling cost	1165	3545	2439	1003
0.2	Document Identification rate (%)	71.64	96.86	93.44	5.88
	False Positive Error Rate (%)	0.67	1.69	1.05	0.35
	False Negative Error Rate (%)	0	0.04	0.01	0.01
	Expert labeling cost	1553	4043	2826	1060
0.3	Document Identification rate (%)	73.28	99.65	94.05	6.73
	False Positive Error Rate (%)	0.41	0.68	0.54	0.1
	False Negative Error Rate (%)	0	0.01	0.0006	0.003
	Expert labeling cost	1872	5562	3913	1313

Table 8.   The similarity threshold effect in the email dataset

Similarity		Min	Max	Mean	Std. Deviation
0.1	Document Identification rate (%)	90.71	99.73	98.02	2.15
	False Positive Error Rate (%)	1.82	3.55	2.58	0.63
	False Negative Error Rate (%)	3.12	11.88	6.85	3.03
	Expert labeling cost	1569	8197	4401	2550
0.15	Document Identification rate (%)	91.46	99.61	98.07	2.04
	False Positive Error Rate (%)	1.24	2.69	1.7	0.38
	False Negative Error Rate (%)	2.47	7.94	5.19	1.74
	Expert labeling cost	2094	10224	5875	3142
0.2	Document Identification rate (%)	89.77	99.72	97.91	2.56
	False Positive Error Rate (%)	0.79	2.24	1.48	0.57
	False Negative Error Rate (%)	1.76	4.93	3.63	0.93
	Expert labeling cost	2986	12412	7828	3724
0.3	Document Identification rate (%)	90.27	99.98	97.47	2.58
	False Positive Error Rate (%)	0.43	1.13	0.62	0.2
	False Negative Error Rate (%)	1.18	1.94	1.8	0.18
	Expert labeling cost	5727	17595	12409	4624

ANOVA has shown a significant increase in the False Positive and False Negative Error Rates with a decrease in the similarity threshold. This can be explained by a decrease in the number of clusters as the similarity threshold becomes lower. Consequently, the clusters become larger and more heterogeneous, resulting in a declining classification performance.

4.5.5. *Time-based analysis*

Figures 1 and 2 show the classification accuracy as a function of time (amount of arriving documents) in the terror and the email datasets, respectively, with the 50% labeling percentage. We define accuracy as the portion of documents identified correctly by the clustering-based classifier out of all incoming documents. The graphs show the difference between two incremental clustering algorithms (Crisp Cosine Clustering vs. Fuzzy Cosine Clustering) and three similarity thresholds (0.10, 0.15, and 0.20).

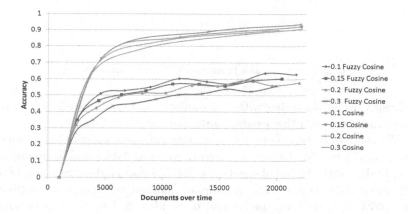

Fig. 1. Accuracy as a function of time in the terror dataset

The X-axis shows the number of incoming documents over time, while the Y-axis shows the percentage of arrived documents we were able to classify correctly using the clusters labeled by the expert. Each point on the graph represents an expert's call when he was asked to label several unlabeled clusters.

We can see that the frequency of expert calls increases as the similarity threshold goes up. This occurs because a higher similarity threshold increases the number of clusters, which in turn requires calling the expert more frequently. The graphs also demonstrate that the crisp cosine clustering results in a higher percentage of correctly identified documents than the fuzzy cosine clustering and that there is no significant difference between the similarity thresholds in terms of accuracy. Thus, based on our results in sub-section 4.5.4 above, the recommended clustering method

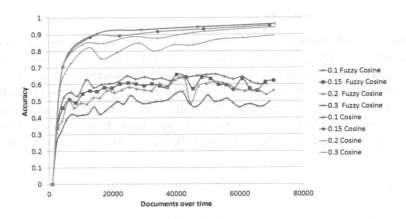

Fig. 2.   Accuracy as a function of time in the email dataset

is Crisp Cosine Clustering with the similarity threshold of 0.2, which is a compromise between the accuracy rate and the FP/FN rates.

We compared the accuracy of our clustering-based algorithm to supervised classifiers. In the terror dataset, we used Weka and a resampling filter to deal with the imbalanced data (21, 528 normal documents and only 582 terror documents). The resampling method is supervised, implying that 100% of arrived documents had to be identified by the expert before choosing equal number of instances from each class. The terror dataset was processed using the J48 classifier with 10-fold cross-validation. We obtained a False Positive Error Rate of 26%, a False Negative Error Rate of 1% and 86.67% of correctly classified instances. The accuracy percentage was lower than obtained when using the ACCA algorithm and the False Positive Error Rate was much higher. In Ref. 20, several supervised algorithms were applied to the same email dataset that we used in this paper. The results showed accuracy rate of 66.7% for SVM and Naïve Bayes, which is considerably lower than the rate we have achieved here.

5. Conclusions

In this paper, we introduced a novel methodology for clustering-based classification of stationary document streams using active learning. The empirical evaluation shows that by using active learning and clustering we can improve the classification rate over time. The proposed method aims at a stream of incoming documents where, in the beginning, all documents are unlabeled. The documents arriving from the stream are clustered and either assigned to an existing cluster or used to start a new cluster. The number of possible clusters is not limited. Occasionally, we call an expert who receives several clusters to label. The expert labels the clusters based on the cluster medoid and all documents in a labeled cluster are assigned the same label. With arrival of more documents and their labeling, we should call the expert less frequently considering the fact that most documents are expected to belong to existing clusters and thus we can identify them automatically without using the services of a human expert.

We have evaluated the algorithm on two document streams from two different domains. The goal of our experiments was to find the fastest way of reaching the point where a high percentage of arriving documents can be categorized correctly without calling an expert. The number of evaluated algorithm settings was 192. The conclusion was that the best setting is to use the Crisp Cosine Clustering algorithm together with either density, size or radius-based cluster choosing strategy and labeling 50% of unlabeled clusters on each expert call. The recommended similarity threshold for clustering is 0.2.

Future research may include evaluation of the proposed method on additional document streams to test the consistency of the trends shown in this work, especially for multi-class text categorization problems. Another research direction may be increasing the number of documents labeled by the expert in each cluster. By labeling additional documents, we may be able to decrease the false negative \positive rates. However, this approach will also increase the total amount of documents labeled by the expert.

We have used crisp cosine clustering and fuzzy cosine clustering as incremental clustering algorithms. In future work, other incremental clustering methods, such as Refs. 24 and 7 may be used. In this work, we have assumed stationarity of the incoming document stream. It would be interesting to develop methods for incremental clustering of non-stationary data streams, where the lexicon and the topic set may change over time. As opposed to a clustering-based classifier, we may use a supervised classification algorithm, such as Naïve Bayes or SVM that will induce a classification model from the data labeled by the expert.

References

1. F. Sebastiani. Machine learning in automated text categorization, *ACM computing surveys (CSUR).* **34**(1), 1–47 (2002).
2. J.-M. Xu, G. Fumera, F. Roli, and Z.-H. Zhou. Training spamassassin with active semi-supervised learning. In *Proceedings of the 6th Conference on Email and Anti-Spam (CEAS09)* (2009).
3. M. Friedman, D. Havazelet, D. Alberg, A. Kandel, and M. Last. A new lexicon-based method for automated detection of terrorist web documents. In eds. S. Singh and M. Singh, *Progress in Pattern Recognition*, pp. 119–128. Springer-Verlag, London (2007).
4. A. Kyriakopoulou and T. Kalamboukis. Text classification using clustering. In *Proceedings of the Discovery Challenge Workshop at ECML/PKDD 2006*, pp. 28–38 (2006).
5. H. T. Nguyen and A. Smeulders. Active learning using pre-clustering. In *Proceedings of the twenty-first international conference on Machine learning*, p. 79 (2004).
6. D. H. Fisher. Knowledge acquisition via incremental conceptual clustering, *Machine learning.* **2**(2), 139–172 (1987).
7. Y. Liu, Q. Guo, L. Yang, and Y. Li. Research on incremental clustering. In *Consumer Electronics, Communications and Networks (CECNet), 2012 2nd International Conference on*, pp. 2803–2806 (2012).
8. A. K. Jain, M. N. Murty, and P. J. Flynn, Data clustering: a review, *ACM computing surveys (CSUR).* **31**(3), 264–323 (1999).
9. M. Friedman, M. Last, O. Zaafrany, M. Schneider, and A. Kandel. A new approach for fuzzy clustering of web documents. In *Fuzzy Systems, 2004. Proceedings. 2004 IEEE International Conference on*, vol. 1, pp. 377–381 (2004).
10. G. Salton, A. Wong, and C.-S. Yang. A vector space model for automatic indexing, *Communications of the ACM.* **18**(11), 613–620 (1975).
11. M. Friedman, M. Last, Y. Makover, and A. Kandel. Anomaly detection in web documents using crisp and fuzzy-based cosine clustering methodology, *Information sciences.* **177**(2), 467–475 (2007).
12. B. Settles. Active learning literature survey, *Machine Learning.* **15**(2), 201–221 (1994).
13. D. D. Lewis and W. A. Gale. A sequential algorithm for training text classifiers. In *Proceedings of the 17th annual international ACM SIGIR conference on Research and development in information retrieval*, pp. 3–12 (1994).
14. A. K. McCallumzy and K. Nigamy. Employing em and pool-based active learning for text classification. In *Proc. International Conference on Machine Learning (ICML)*, pp. 359–367 (1998).
15. I. Žliobaitė, A. Bifet, B. Pfahringer, and G. Holmes. Active learning with drifting streaming data, *IEEE transactions on neural networks and learning systems.* **25**(1), 27–39 (2014).
16. J. Kranjc, J. Smailović, V. Podpečan, M. Grčar, M. Žnidaršič, and N. Lavrač. Active learning for sentiment analysis on data streams: Methodology and

workflow implementation in the clowdflows platform, *Information Processing & Management.* **51**(2), 187–203 (2015).

17. A. Kyriakopoulou and T. Kalamboukis. Combining clustering with classification for spam detection in social bookmarking systems. In *Proceedings of European Conference on Machine Learning and Principles and Practice of Knowledge Discovery in Databases Discovery Challenge, (ECML/PKDD RSDC 2008)*, pp. 47–54 (2008).

18. C. Wemmert, G. Forestier, and S. Derivaux. Improving supervised learning with multiple clusterings. In *Applications of Supervised and Unsupervised Ensemble Methods*, pp. 135–149. Springer (2009).

19. H. T. Nguyen and A. Smeulders. Active learning using pre-clustering. In *Proceedings of the Twenty-first International Conference on Machine Learning*, ICML '04, pp. 79–, ACM, New York, NY, USA (2004). ISBN 1-58113-838-5. doi: 10.1145/1015330.1015349. URL http://doi.acm.org/10.1145/1015330.1015349.

20. D. DeBarr and H. Wechsler. Spam detection using clustering, random forests, and active learning. In *Sixth Conference on Email and Anti-Spam. Mountain View, California* (2009).

21. P. D. Turney. Learning algorithms for keyphrase extraction, *Information Retrieval.* **2**(4), 303–336 (2000).

22. M. Friedman, A. Kandel, M. Schneider, M. Last, B. Shapira, Y. Elovici, and O. Zaafrany. A fuzzy-based algorithm for web document clustering. In *Fuzzy Information, 2004. Processing NAFIPS'04. IEEE Annual Meeting of the*, vol. 2, pp. 524–527 (2004).

23. A. Bifet, J. Read, I. Žliobaitė, B. Pfahringer, and G. Holmes. Pitfalls in benchmarking data stream classification and how to avoid them. In *Joint European Conference on Machine Learning and Knowledge Discovery in Databases*, pp. 465–479 (2013).

24. M. Charikar, C. Chekuri, T. Feder, and R. Motwani. Incremental clustering and dynamic information retrieval. In *Proceedings of the Twenty-ninth Annual ACM Symposium on Theory of Computing*, pp. 626–635 (1997).

Chapter 6

Supporting the Mining of Big Data by Means of Domain Knowledge During the Pre-mining Phases

Rémon Cornelisse[*] and Sunil Choenni[*,†]

[*]*Research and Documentation Centre (WODC), Ministry of Security and Justice, The Hague, The Netherlands*
[†]*Rotterdam University of Applied Science, Rotterdam, The Netherlands*

The selection and pre-processing of data are key activities in the interpretation and extraction of knowledge from data streams. Their role become even more crucial in the context of big data mining where huge amounts of (volatile) data from various types are normal, and simply storing all data is not only becoming infeasible but also undesired. This makes the exploitation of domain knowledge the key ingredient to properly reduce the data stream while simultaneously keep information loss to a minimum. Using several examples from the completely different fields of cyber security, astronomy (in particular the detection of exoplanets), criminal justice (in particular in the Netherlands) and cyber security the importance of domain knowledge is illustrated. For each of these examples time series analysis is the goal, but the challenges during the selection and pre-processing stages are completely different. However, despite the differences, two different, but related, trends can be distinguished. The first trend shows that steps that need to be emphasized during pre-processing depend on the consistency of the time series data, and the second trend shows a shift from optimizing the records included in the time series data to optimizing the approach taken to allow the data to be mined.

1. Introduction

According to IBM, about 2.5 Exabyte ($=2.5 \times 10^{18}$ bytes) of data is produced every day,[1] and this is still growing exponentially. This is affecting almost all facets of society, ranging from science (e.g. CERN, genome project, etc.) via the monitoring of processes (e.g. the weather, manufacturing, etc.) to social life (e.g. social media, video streaming, etc.) However, this growth is also creating daunting challenges, not only in the collection, storage and access of such large data streams, but also the processing and interpretation. Such large data streams, and the problems surrounding them, are typically referred to as big data.

Big data is either defined as a term for i) a vague metaphor for solving complicated problems with data or ii) data that cannot be handled with conventional tools.[2] Commonly, big data is characterized by the '3Vs', i.e. high volume, high velocity and/or high variety,[3] but other words starting with 'V' are sometimes also included (e.g. value, veracity, etc.)[4] High volume indicates the large quantity of data involved. High velocity is the speed at which data is created, while the high variety indicates the large variety of data types involved (e.g. structured databases, images, text, audio, etc.).

Each phase of big data has its own challenges and is leading to new developments.[5] Since the storage of the Terabytes of data is non-trivial, big data is driving recent developments in storage technology. Another technological problem is the increasing fraction of potentially interesting data that can never be analyzed due to the huge amounts of data that are collected.[6] Furthermore, the sheer variety of non-traditional data (e.g. unstructured data, audio or video files, etc.) provides new processing challenges.[7] Finally, averting privacy breaches, due to the combining of different data streams, is another challenge.[8,9]

The goal of big data is to extract information to enable enhanced decision making, insight discovery or process optimization,[10] and this is done with data mining. This field also shows many new developments and challenges due to big data. For example, the advances in distributed computing (such as MapReduce and Hadoop) have been driven by big data,[5] while cloud computing allows data mining without the need to invest in expensive infrastructure.[11] Furthermore, creating and maintaining a process that extracts and transforms relevant information from the original sources for analyses is a continuous challenge.[7] Another challenge for big data is interpreting the results and making them understood by the decision makers. This not only includes understanding how a result was obtained, but also develop a way to visualize the results in an intuitive way.

The big data and mining challenges get compounded when the time component is important. For example, due to concept drift statistical properties in a data stream can change over time[12] (e.g. trending topics on Twitter, but also periodic seasonal variations). Another related challenge is the duration of the life cycles of the phenomenon that could be present in the data stream. A final example is the challenge to visualize the information that is continuously extracted from the data streams. Presenting such data over both large and very short timescales simultaneously requires new visualization techniques.[13]

In this chapter the challenges with big data during the selection and pre-processing stages of the mining process are discussed. This is illustrated with three real-life examples from very different fields that all have a strong time component, namely: astronomy, criminal justice and cyber security. It will be shown that each case has its own unique challenges that are mainly motivated by domain knowledge. Section 2 presents an outline of the different phases in data mining, and paints a broad picture of the problems during the Selection stage (Sect. 2.1) and the pre-processing stage (Sect. 2.2). Section 3 presents the challenges for the astronomy case, Sect. 4 those for the criminal justice system, and Sect. 5 those for the Cyber Security case. In Sect. 6 the different cases are compared and their differences and similarities are discussed with regard to domain knowledge (Sect. 6.1) and the presence of the time component (Sect. 6.2). Finally, in Sect. 7 the conclusions are presented.

2. The Pre-mining Phases

To mine data streams it is important to take the process of Knowledge Discovery in Databases (KDD) into account. Knowledge Discovery is defined as "the non-trivial process of identifying valid, novel, potentially useful, and ultimately understandable patterns in data",[14] and is an iterative process that consist of multiple stages. Although the approaches that have been outlined by KDD have been refined over years, e.g. in the form of CRISP[15] or SEMMA,[16] nine steps can in essence be recognized, which can be summarized in 5 more general stages:

(1) Selection
     (a) Developing and understanding the application domain
     (b) Creating a target dataset/data stream
(2) Pre-processing
     (c) Data cleaning and pre-processing
(3) Transformation
     (d) Data reduction and projection
(4) Data mining
     (e) Choosing the data mining task
     (f) Choosing the data mining algorithm
     (g) Data mining
(5) Interpretation/Evaluation
     (h) Interpreting
     (i) Consolidating discovered knowledge.

Nowadays the term data mining has a very broad meaning, and is used for almost every exercise that tries to extract information.[17] This can range from a pure statistical analysis where the dataset, the model and the goal are all very well defined to a completely blind search for patterns in an unknown data stream. In practice, most data mining exercises are in between these extremes, and (some) ideas about the content of the datasets and the goal of the data mining are known beforehand.

Since most data mining exercises have an idea about the goal, the first two stages of KDD are crucial for a successful campaign. These stages, the focus of this chapter, become even more important when it is not possible to store all data or the data has a time component. Since it is often difficult to explore the original data stream for potential features when a time component is involved,[18] the selection criteria and pre-processing procedures must typically be developed before the target data stream can even be created. In the remainder of this section the first two steps of KDD are described in a more general way.

2.1. *The Selection Stage*

The goal of the "Developing and understanding the application domain" step is to obtain feeling for the main issues in the application domain to identify a well defined problem. Typically this problem needs to be broken down in many sub-questions, lead to the identification of new issues that need to be solved. For example, a common problem in Cyber Security is: "How can malicious intrusions be detected in high-speed network traffic in real-time without causing noticeable delays (by the users of the network)." An obvious sub-question is: "What are malicious intrusions?" which leads to the question of: "What does a specific malicious intrusion (e.g. certain malware) look like?"

Obviously, the fact that the main problem is divided into a set of sub-questions does not mean that these are less important. On the contrary, it is only by answering all these sub-questions that a data mining exercise can be developed to find a solution for the main problem. However, one thing to guard against is losing sight of the main problem. In general, it is better to only answer the smallest set of questions that still meet the minimum requirements to answer the main problem. Afterwards, aspects that could still need further clarification can be identified, and if needed a new data mining problem can be formulated.

One thing to note is that typically more in-depth domain knowledge is needed when the sub-question becomes more specific. This leads to a better understanding of the application domain, leading to a better formulation of the higher level questions or even the main problem. If a question has finally been divided in a set of sub-questions that cannot be further broken down, its optimal solution is usually evident. At this point it is time to start thinking about creating the target data stream.

During stage 2 the optimal solution to each sub-question is formulated. Some of these solutions could be as simple as selecting a specific value from a single attribute or a combination of attributes. However, due to all kinds of different constraints, the optimal solution is not always feasible. For example, it is not possible to directly measure the required attribute needed, or it could take too much bandwidth or processing time to make the solution feasible. In this case a sub-optimal solution or even a trade-off needs to be found that will still achieve the minimum requirements to answer the question. Also, it could be possible that with the available data stream it is impossible to answer the question. In this case the underlying question, or in the worst case the main problem, will need to be re-phrased. When it is clear that all sub-questions can be answered with the data streams that are available for mining, all necessary attributes can be collected to create the target data stream.

Using again the Cyber security example, where two different kinds of malicious software need to be detected real-time without causing any noticeable delay to the network traffic, the considerations during the Selection phase can be illustrated. The first kind of software is a 'simple' piece of malware that redirects a user to a malicious website (which is located at a specific IP address). For this malware the optimal solution is to monitor if this IP address (website) is being accessed by outgoing network traffic. Since checking a common attribute in the network data, the destination IP addresses of the outgoing traffic, provides the solution, it is simple to implement. On the other hand, the second piece of malicious software is a more advanced piece of malware, and the simplest solution for its detection is to search for a certain signature. However, if this malware is hidden in an encrypted communication (thereby making the signature undetectable), or embedded in file that is too large to scan in depth without large delays in the network traffic, the simplest solution becomes unfeasible. The trade-off could be that the detection is not done real-time anymore or that a noticeable delay occurs in the network traffic. Which trade-off will be made depends if the real-time or the delay aspect is considered more important. If it is acceptable that potentially malicious pieces of software are first quarantined and carefully checked, the original question could then be re-phrased into: 'How can malware be detected in quasi real-time without causing any noticeable delays to the remaining network traffic?'

2.2. *The Pre-processing Stage*

Real data typically has many shortcomings, and raw data is therefore considered 'dirty'. For example, a data stream can be incomplete, noisy, inconsistent, and can be incoherent when multiple data streams are involved. The goal of the pre-processing stage is to transform this 'dirty' data into a consistent and understandable 'clean 'data stream. To create such a 'clean' data stream the steps that are carried out are: i) combine the data from the different data streams into a coherent one, ii) fill in missing values, iii) resolve inconsistencies, iv) understand the noise components.

Combining data from different data streams can be challenging. For example, attributes in different data streams could have the same name, but this does not guarantee a similar meaning. There might be subtle (or not so subtle) differences, which have to be taken into account. The opposite problem, where similar attributes have different names, can also occur.[19,20] Furthermore, combining the noise characteristics of each data stream and determining how they propagate in the combined set might not be trivial. Finally, even if the attributes of different data streams might have a similar meaning, it does not guarantee that they have the same unit. An example is the different measurement systems that are used, such as the metric, United States customary units and the Imperial system (e.g. liter vs. US gallon vs. imperial gallon).

Although it is not always possible, sometimes there are ways to fill in missing values.[21] One such method is to replace a value with one from a similar attribute. Another way to fill in missing values is to infer the mean, or most probable, value from relevant attributes. Although these methods appear similar there is a significant difference. In the first method a replacement value is directly taken from a different attribute, while in the second method a value must be derived from one or more different attributes.

Inconsistencies are common in data streams and can have many origins. For example, they occur due to human errors such as typing mistakes (e.g. entries with 981 as the year of birth) that are introduced in the database. Other common inconsistencies can occur due to the reluctance to fill out (apparently) unnecessary paperwork that the system insists on. Generally some generic or nonsense input is given to comply with the demand of input. Another form of inconsistency occurs when developments in the real world cannot accurately be taken into account by the database, leading to new set of values that do not correspond with the original definition of an attribute. A final form of inconsistency occurs when there are multiple ways to represent the same object. For example, a typical Dutch last name is 'van Dijk', which can also be written in a database as 'v. Dijk', 'Dijk, van', 'van Dyk', etc.

Finally, understanding the noise characteristics of the data stream and how they propagate can be crucial for certain mining problems. In general, the following four kinds of noise can be distinguished. 1) Spurious noise, i.e. outliers that can clearly not be correct (e.g. a person that is 1035 years old, i.e. was born in 981). 2) Noise due to measurement errors (intrinsic to all measuring devices). 3) Systematic noise due to a systemic off-set in the measuring device. 4) Background noise due to presence of extraneous sources that cannot be separated from the object is mined. Understanding the importance of each noise component, and their effect on the confidence of the final answer, can be crucial.

3. Case I: Astrophysics

The astrophysics case is illustrated by the Kepler satellite mission to detect Earth-sized exoplanets (see Ref. 22 for an overview of the results), i.e. planets around stars other than our sun. The mining question can be summarized as: 'How common are Earth-sized exoplanets?' Although high level of domain knowledge is needed to successfully answer this question, there are large deviations from the steps presented in the previous section. These deviations will be discussed, but the emphasis will be on steps where domain knowledge is crucial.

3.1. *The Selection Stage*

The largest deviation from the steps described in the previous section is at the beginning. Since no time series data existed to detect of Earth-sized exoplanets prior to Kepler, one needed to be created via a dedicated (scientific) program. This allows for the creation of a perfectly optimized time series data, instead of the more common situation where the time series data were never intended to answer the specific mining question.

The first step is to break down the main question into more specific sub-questions, and could, for example, be: 1) How many stars need to be observed to give a meaningful answer to the prevalence of exoplanets?, 2) How to rule out alternative explanations of the data?, 3) How can Earth-sized exoplanets be detected? These major questions do not have an obvious optimal solution yet, and need to be broken down further. Furthermore, these major questions are also strongly dependent on each other, since the answer to one major question will strongly influence the answer to the other major questions.

To continue the example, the third major question can be further divided into the following three (related) questions: 1) What is the most promising technique to detect exoplanets? 2) What is the minimum precision needed to detect an Earth-sized exoplanet? 3) How to reach this minimum precision? The first of these questions does have an obvious answer to any domain expert, and directly provides the answer to the second of these questions. However, it will create multiple new subquestions for the third of these questions, while also indicating how the other major questions can be further broken down.

For Kepler the most promising technique to create time series data to search for Earth-like exoplanets was transit photometry. With this technique the brightness of a star is continuously measured, and when a planet crosses between the observer and the star there is a small drop in the amount of light. Using the Earth-Sun system as a benchmark, the minimum requirements can be calculated to be able to detect an Earth-like exoplanet. For a far-away observer the Earth passes in front of the Sun once every year for a duration of 13 hours, leading to a drop in brightness of 0.0084%. Since the drop needs to be measurable, the total noise on each individual measurement needs to be smaller (for Kepler 0.002% was chosen). However, observations with such a small noise contribution are not feasible from Earth (where at best a drop of at least 0.1% can be measured), leaving only a satellite mission as the alternative to create such time series data.

A satellite mission adds a lot of new requirements to the nature of the data that can be collected. For example, a satellite mission has only a limited lifetime (for Kepler the nominal lifetime was 3.5 years), constraining the time to create time series data that can answer the main question. Furthermore, there is only a limited amount of bandwidth to send information back to Earth. Therefore, the pre-processing at the satellite must be done carefully, since not everything can be reproduced on the ground. Also, satellite missions are expensive and major modifications are typically impossible after launch. This means that before the first data is even collected, all potential issues that prohibit the answer to the main problem must be solved. For Kepler these problems are, for example, getting the total noise contribution to a small enough level, making sure that the duration of the time series data is large enough that alternative explanations for many transits can be excluded, while still being able to give an answer to the occurrence rate of Earth-like exoplanets. In Refs. 23 and 24 an overview of the main issues and the solutions for the Kepler satellite mission are sketched.

3.2. *The Pre-processing Stage*

For the creation of the Kepler time series data many of the steps in Sect. 2.2 can be skipped. For example, since the time series data is specifically created to solve the mining question, it is not necessary to combine data from different data streams. Also the filling in of missing values and the resolving of inconsistencies can be skipped. Unless a glitch occurred on-board the satellite (making all data during that period suspect, and should be discarded), no missing values or inconsistencies occur. However, understanding the noise characteristics is crucial to its success.

The importance of understanding the noise is illustrated in Fig. 1, where the (fictive) observations of a transit, with the same characteristics as the Earth passing in front of the Sun, are shown. Although the measurements are all the same, the noise decreases from the top to bottom panel. The top panel shows the best that can be done from Earth, i.e. it is not possible to distinguish the transit due to the noise. In the middle panel the noise is similar to the depth of the transit. Although there is a hint that the brightness is dimming, the noise is still too large to make a convincing argument. The bottom panel shows the transit with similar noise characteristics as Kepler, and now there is a clear dip.

Since the noise characteristics play such an important role in answering the main mining question, a complete understanding of each source of noise is necessary before the experiment was devised. Some forms of noise could not be controlled, such as the intrinsic variability of a star. There are no stars where the brightness is completely stable, but some types of stars are more stable than others. Therefore, the knowledge which stars are most stable is important, especially since these stars already needed to be selected beforehand (since the bandwidth for the data transfer to earth does not allow the observation of all stars).

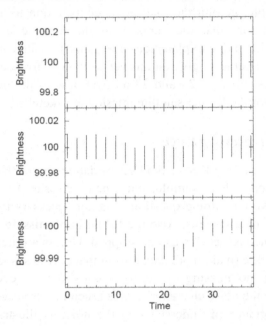

Figure 1: Examples of the same (fictive) transit observed with different noise characteristics. In the top panel the noise is similar to the best that can be done from Earth, in the middle panel the noise is similar to the dip, and in the bottom the noise level is four times smaller than the dip.

Another source that cannot be controlled is the amount of shot noise due to the counting of light particles (i.e. photons). The exact size of this noise contribution depends only on the brightness of a star, i.e. fainter stars have a higher uncertainty, and should not be included in the list of observed stars. However, to obtain a reliable measure of the occurrence rate of Earth-like exoplanets, enough stars need to be included in the sample. The only way to increase this sample is to increase the mirror (i.e. allows the inclusion of fainter stars) or increasing the part of the sky that is observed (i.e. allows the inclusion of stars that were previously outside the field of view). However, such changes are challenging and will have consequences for other sources of noise.

Finally, there is a large range of noise sources that can be controlled as much as possible, such as the detector, electronics, the instability of the spacecraft, thermal noise, optical noise or stray light, but also the background noise. This background noise is always present, but depends strongly on the chosen satellite orbit. However, changing the orbit leads to all kinds of changes to the possible design of the spacecraft. In total, every design choice changes the contribution of each noise component. Understanding the way these contributions are connected was essential for the successful design of Kepler and needed to be done before the first data could be obtained.

4. Case II: Criminal Justice System

The second case is about the criminal justice system in the Netherlands, and has completely different challenges during the pre-mining phases than the first case. The goal of the criminal justice system is to uphold the enforcement of law and the public safety of the people, via an effective and efficient system and administration. However, the system is composed of many interdependent agencies (e.g. police, public prosecution, the courts, etc.), that all have a strong tradition of independence. Furthermore, each agency has its own task and information needs, which they register in their own information system, hampering an efficient exchange of information.[25,26] Here the problems and pitfalls are illustrated when the information systems of the different agencies are combined. Although many different mining questions can be formulated, the focus will be on the efficiency of the system as a whole in order to find the different bottlenecks.

4.1. *The Selection Stage*

The question 'What is the elapsed time for moving completely through the criminal justice system in the Netherlands?' sounds straightforward.

For example, for the sub-question 'What are the different parts in the system?', most people think of the following linear chain:

(crime) → investigate → prosecute → trial → execute sentence → (case close)

However, Fig. 2 shows that the flow scheme of only the first part of the chain is already more complicated. In practice many side chains, short cuts, and loop backs occur in the criminal justice system. For example, Fig. 2 shows that during the investigation phase the police interacts with other agencies (which are indicated by the yellow boxes). Furthermore, when the police finishes the investigation, it has more than options for the next step than just moving on to the prosecution (the green box), most of which are part of the execution of the sentence phase (red boxes). For example, for small crimes the police in the Netherlands is allowed to directly pass sentence (i.e. penalty by the police) or come to an understanding with the suspect about a fitting sentence without going to court (i.e. police transaction).

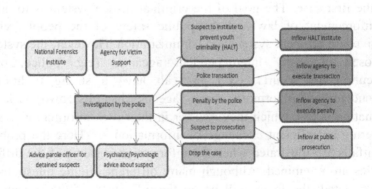

Figure 2: Simplified flow scheme for the first part in the criminal justice system of the Netherlands.

The simplified flow scheme in Fig. 2 also shows that a typical elapsed time through the system does not exist.[25] Knowledge about all the possible paths through the chains is needed to answer the sub-question 'What are the different chains in the system?' Since there are a large number of routes through the system, only the most common ones can be explored in detail, and somehow these need to be selected.

Another question that the main one can be broken into is: 'What is meant by elapsed time?' For example, is the elapsed time for someone sentenced to imprisonment measured until the beginning or the end of the time in detention, or even until the end of the time on parole? Another example is when the sentence is a fine. Is the elapsed time in this case the moment that the collection agency has send a bill, a bailiff is send, the fine is partially paid, or the fine is fully paid? A final example is the elapsed time for a convict that is sentenced to both detention and community service. Is the elapsed time measured after finishing both imposed sanctions or for each sanction separately? If the second case is chosen, should one take into account the duration of the other sanction? Again, a basic understanding of the criminal justice system in the Netherlands is needed to get optimal answers.

4.2. *The Pre-processing Stage*

During the pre-processing of the data streams of the criminal justice system the first 3 steps described in Sect. 2.2 are the most important. Although some though is given to the noise characteristics, only spurious noise needs consideration. However, due to the large size of the data stream and the kind of mining questions, outliers can in general be ignored.

As illustrated in Fig. 2, data from over a dozen independent agencies, all with their own data information system, need to be combined. This is complicated due to the way information is registered at the different agencies. For example, for the police a case corresponds to a criminal offense (which can have multiple persons involved), while it corresponds to an unique person for the public prosecutor (which can be suspected of multiple crimes). Furthermore, there is the added constraint of privacy regulations, which makes it impossible to use any sensitive personal information attributes, and the joining needs to be done via a so-called case identifier (e.g. the number the public prosecution assigns to the case of a suspect). However, this case identifier is not always properly registered for the agencies that are concerned with the execution of a sentence (since it is not considered relevant). Therefore, in the information systems of these agencies it happens that only nonsense is recorded for the case identifier. This makes the tracing of a unique person through the criminal justice chain complicated.

Another problem is the definition of the attributes registered by the different agencies. Seemingly similar attributes could have different meanings. For example, in the Netherlands there is an agency that coordinates the execution of sentences and several agencies that actually carry them out. One would expect that the start date a sentence is executed is similar for both the coordinating and executing agency, but this is not always the case. Only by detailed knowledge of all information systems is it possible to select the correct date to measure the elapsed time in the case of, for example, a community service.

Another issue that is encountered is that different data streams have a different value for the same attribute. For example, each data stream records the date of the verdict, and somehow this value is not always the same between data streams. Since the correct date cannot be determined from the registered data alone, one of the conflicting dates has to be chosen. In this case, knowledge about how this date is registered in each system is needed to determine which date has the highest probability to be correct. The opposite, missing values that are only recorded in a single data stream, also occurs. In this case rules are needed on how to impute such missing value. For example, from experience it is known that most crimes are reported on the same day as they are committed. When the date a crime is committed is not recorded, the reported date could be used.

A major problem with the data streams in the criminal justice system is that they are manually filled, dramatically increasing the changes of a mistake. Fortunately, due to the abundance of data streams it is possible to include many safety checks to catch these mistakes. For example, for elapsed times the goal is to obtain a sequence of important dates to measure the time differences. If one of these dates in the sequence is anomalous this will be easy to catch. However, although the mistake is found it is typically not possible to correct, and it must be accepted that not all elapsed times can be measured.

A common complication for the criminal justice system is the fast pace at which definitions change. For example, due to legal reform existing laws could change meaning or could even be repealed. In particular when monitoring the elapsed time for a specific offense through time, these legal changes need to be taken into account to make sure that same offense (or at least a closely related one) is used. A similar kind of change is the reclassification of the different judicial districts. For example, courts could be closed to save money or the exact boundaries of the districts could change to better divide the workload. In particular when the elapsed times of specific districts are monitored these changes can lead to a structural break in the trend.

A related problem is the shift in the severity rating of an offense. For all kinds of reasons the penalty for an offense could change. For example, offenses for which the typical sentence used to be imprisonment could change into a fine or community service. In particular when the type of penalty changes there is large influence on the elapsed time, making comparison with previous periods impossible. Finally, the introduction (or disappearance) of new penalties will have impact on the duration of the elapsed times. For example, in the Netherlands the public prosecution is nowadays allowed to pass sentence over certain offenses, thereby bypassing the judge and dramatically shortening the elapsed time.

5. Case III: Cyber Security

The final case, cyber security, is a very broad topic and to limit the scope the focus will be on the more specialized topic of network forensics.[27] The goal of network forensics is the capture, recording and analysis of network events in order to discover the source of security attacks, anomalous behavior in network traffic or other problem incidents. The main challenge of network forensics is that it has to deal with large amounts of volatile and dynamic information that will otherwise be lost.

5.1. *The Selection Stage*

The first step in network forensics is the capture and recording of network traffic. One way to do this is to capture and store all network data and the analysis happens afterwards. However, this requires large amounts of storage space, in particular with traffic over a long period of time. Furthermore, finding important information in such a large amount of data is challenging. The alternative is to analyze traffic in real-time and only store information that could be useful. This technique has the disadvantages that a good processor is needed for the real-time analysis, beforehand it is decided which information needs to be kept, while it can still lead to large amounts of stored data. Afterwards, both techniques still require that the (large amount of) stored network data is optimized for network forensics purposes. Therefore, the central mining question can be 'How to reduce and improve the amount of stored network traffic data to optimize network forensics analyses?'

The main problem has been formulated in such a way that it immediately raises new questions. For example, 1) 'What is meant by reduce and improve?', 2) 'What are typical analyses carried out by network forensics?', or 3) 'What network data needs to be stored?' are several obvious questions. Some of these questions apply for network forensics in general (e.g. question 1), but others (e.g. question 2) depend on local constrains. For example, the software tools available at a company limit the types of possible analyses. Finally, for some questions the answers depend on external factors, e.g. question 3, such as national privacy laws that dictate the kind of information to be stored (and how).

The questions from the previous paragraph are related. Depending on the kind of analyses needed, different kinds of network data have to be stored. For example, the analyses of email traffic needs different data than checking for breaches via a vulnerability in a web form, leading to completely different ways to reduce and improve the stored data. This implies that the mining question is too broad and needs more focus. Although this re-focusing of the mining question was done for illustrative purposes, it also happens when domain understanding increases.

For the remainder of this case the focus will be on NetFlow data,[28] i.e. 'How to reduce the amount of stored NetFlow data while simultaneously optimizing for network forensics analyses?' NetFlow is a high-level description of the network traffic that registers where the traffic is coming from, where it is going and how much is generated (but not the content of the data). Figure 3 shows example output. For each flow the sending and destination IP address, the ports that were used (e.g. port 80 is typically used for http traffic), the start time and duration, the

Date first seen	Duration	Proto	Src IP Addr: Port		Dst IP Addr: Port	Packets	Bytes	Flows
2014-02-05 11:04:21.472	2.880	TCP	0.0.0.01:80	->	0.0.0.02:51321	18	11865	1
2014-02-05 11:04:21.536	2.816	TCP	0.0.0.02:51322	->	0.0.0.01:80	31	13317	1
2014-02-05 11:04:21.536	2.816	TCP	0.0.0.01:80	->	0.0.0.02:51323	5	2994	1
2014-02-05 11:04:21.920	0.960	TCP	0.0.0.03:50696	->	0.0.0.04:443	3	152	1
2014-02-05 11:04:05.152	20.480	TCP	0.0.0.05:50560	->	0.0.006:80	41	53489	1
2014-02-05 11:04:21.472	3.072	TCP	0.0.0.02:51320	->	0.0.0.01:80	27	14848	1
2014-02-05 11:04:21.472	2.880	TCP	0.0.0.01:80	->	0.0.0.02:51320	24	16081	1
2014-02-05 11:04:21.536	3.008	TCP	0.0.0.02:51323	->	0.0.0.01:80	7	3742	1
2014-02-05 11:04:22.112	0.256	TCP	0.0.0.07:49168	->	0.0.0.08:524	2	110	1
2014-02-05 11:04:13.664	9.024	TCP	0.0.0.09:50074	->	0.0.0.01:80	14	5101	1
2014-02-05 11:04:21.856	0.768	TCP	0.0.0.10:443	->	0.0.0.11:37578	5	2904	1
2014-02-05 11:04:13.984	8.576	TCP	0.0.0.12:50567	->	0.0.0.14:443	4	5073	1
2014-02-05 11:04:14.240	8.448	TCP	0.0.0.15:443	->	0.0.0.16:49559	4	525	1
2014-02-05 11:04:14.112	8.384	TCP	0.0.0.16:49559	->	0.0.0.15:443	3	2185	1
2014-02-05 11:04:22.240	0.064	TCP	0.0.0.17:80	->	0.0.0.02:51230	4	334	1
2014-02-05 11:04:23.454	3.072	TCP	0.0.0.18.15826	->	0.0.0.19:50026	3	168	1
2014-02-05 11:04:23.454	3.264	TCP	0.0.0.19:50026	->	0.0.0.18:15826	2	89	1
2014-02-05 11:04:26.334	0.000	UDP	0.0.0.20:51142	->	0.0.0.21:53	1	68	1

Summary: total flows: 20, total bytes: 135582, total packets: 203, avg bps: 4904, avg pps: 9, avg bpp:667
Time window: 2014-02-05 11:03:51 – 2014-02-05 11:09:59
Total flows processed: 20150, Blocks skipped: 0, Bytes read: 1047940
Sys: 0.009s flows/second: 2015403.1 Wall: 0.005s flows/second: 3774822.0

Figure 3: Example output of NetFlow data. Note that the Source (Src IP Addr) and Destination IP (Dst IP Addr) addresses have been anonymized for privacy reasons.

communication protocol and the number of bytes are recorded. A typical communication is made up of multiple flows, and NetFlow provides an overview of the traffic (see Ref. 29 for an overview of NetFlow). Combined with information from other sources that have probed the transferred data, NetFlow data is used for Network Forensics purposes.[30] However, domain knowledge is again essential to extract information from NetFlow data that it is useful for network forensics.

5.2. *The Pre-processing Stage*

Although most steps described in Sect. 2.2 need consideration, many of the discussed issues are not relevant due to the standardized format of NetFlow data. For example, inconsistencies are not an issue, and human-made errors cannot occur. Furthermore, the definition of the attributes in the NetFlow data is always the same, and each recorded flow should always have all attributes (i.e. there are no missing values). Although the pre-processing of NetFlow data is similar to the astrophysics case in Sect. 3, there are differences due to the general, multi-purpose, format of NetFlow (instead of the unique format used in Sect. 3).

Typically, since NetFlow data is collected at different points (routers) in the network before it is combined, there must be a guarantee that network traffic from all locations is captured and any overlap in data streams is known. Therefore, a good understanding of the network layout of the organization is needed to make sure that no part is missing or double recorded.

Although the problem of missing attributes is not an issue with NetFlow data, the sampling of the data needs consideration. With high-speed networks it is possible that the NetFlow collector cannot handle the large data stream, leading to drop outs. This is mitigated by setting a sampling rate, i.e. measuring only a fraction of the packets to determine the characteristics of each flow. However, only the characteristics of the measured packets are added to the relevant flow in this case, causing most short communications (consisting of only a few packets) to be missed. Also, since the size and arrival time of individual packets varies a lot, the exact total size and number of packets for each flow is also unknown. Obviously, this can have consequences during the mining and one needs to be aware that sampling has occurred.

Although the typical inconsistencies discussed in Sect. 2.2 do not occur in NetFlow data, it is still necessary to be aware of issues with the ICT infrastructure of the organization. For example, major software upgrades, the introduction of new software packages or the replacement of hardware might lead to different/new features in the network traffic. Being aware of these changes will limit the risk of false warnings, and thereby the amount of unnecessary work.

Background noise is an important pre-processing issue for NetFlow data, in particular when optimizing for network forensics. Since the majority of the large volumes of highly dynamic and volatile network traffic is completely innocuous, it can be regarded as background noise for network forensics purposes. Preferentially this innocuous traffic should be removed before the mining starts, but a good understanding of network traffic (in general and specific for that network) is needed to determine what constitutes innocuous traffic.

6. Domain Knowledge

The challenges during the pre-mining stages were presented for three cases covering very diverse domains (i.e. astrophysics, criminal justice and cyber security), and the importance of domain knowledge was discussed. For each case it is obvious that domain knowledge plays a key role during the selection stage, but beforehand it was less obvious that also for the pre-processing stage each case has its own challenges where domain knowledge plays an important and central role.

6.1. *The Pre-processing Spectrum*

For the astrophysics case, a question is formulated and all potential problems encountered need to be solved before a single piece of data exists to answer it. However, as soon as data is produced, it is always automatically generated in the same, optimized, format. Such a set-up is common for problems in many natural science fields such as physics, earth science, chemistry, etc. Only after a significant investment in time, energy and/or money an experiment is developed to create dedicated time series data to answer the question. The most common pre-processing steps are avoided with such a dedicated time series data, and the emphasis is on understanding the noise characteristics. Such emphasis on noise is common for most natural science problems, since otherwise the question was already answered with previous generation instrumentation, and the experiment would not have been constructed.

The criminal justice example shows the other extreme. Here, several, more or less, unrelated data streams already exist to support tasks at the operational level of the different organizations, and need to be combined to provide insight at the strategic level. This is the typical situation for companies that want to use data mining to improve their efficiency. A significant amount of the pre-processing is used to combine attributes from data streams that are filled by hand and were never designed to answer strategic level questions. Therefore, the emphasis is on understanding the definition of the attributes and the meaning of their values to find out what is relevant, rubbish or has changed over time.

The cyber security example sits in between the previous cases. Like the astrophysics case, data is automatically generated and will always have a specified format. However, now the format has not been optimized for the problem at hand, but is a generally accepted standard. Stock market analysis and traffic control monitoring are other examples where data in such a standard format is generated. Not surprisingly, during the pre-processing phase of such data streams, the problems discussed for the other two cases play a role, but less severe. In other words, understanding the noise characteristics to increase the changes of finding a relevant signature, combined with a good understanding of the definition of each attribute and its range of values, is essential.

The three cases presented show a range in consistency of the time series data that are used. Ranging from the low consistency human-filled time series data of the criminal justice system, via the standard format time series data of the cyber security case, to the dedicated time series data of astrophysics with a high consistency. This also corresponds with a shifting importance of the specific pre-processing steps needed. When consistency is low the importance of the noise contribution is negligible compared to the trustworthiness of each value (i.e. is it relevant, rubbish, and has its meaning changed). When consistency is high it is unlikely that a recorded value is erroneous or has a different meaning, but the contribution of the noise to each data point becomes central.

6.2. *Time-Series Data*

All three cases were chosen because their main question contains a time component. For the astrophysics and criminal justice cases their final goals are time series analyses, while for the cyber security case it is the classification of large volumes of data. Although the actual data mining stage is not discussed here, the time component does add extra constraints during the pre-mining stages.

During the selection stage the impact of the dynamic or timing aspect needs to be developed and understood. Especially since the impact can differ at a fundamental level, even if the mining exercise is very similar. For example, for the astrophysics case the kind questions for the selection stage to create the time series are: 'How many stars need to be simultaneously observed?', 'What types of stars have a low intrinsic variability?', and 'What types of stars are more suitable to harbor an Earth-like exoplanet?' All these questions are related to determining the candidates to include in the time series data. For the criminal justice system on the other hand, the final time series for the mining exercise are created from the different data streams of the partners in the chain. Here, typical questions are: 'What are typical paths through the chain?', 'What is meant by elapsed time?', and 'Does one follow an offence or the offender through the chain?' These questions are about optimizing the approach to building the time series, and are fundamentally different than the ones for the astrophysics case. Despite the fact that the two cases have a similar mining problem, these fundamental differences illustrate that domain knowledge is already essential at the early stages of the mining process.

The timing and dynamic aspects also add extra considerations during the pre-processing stage. Foremost is the problem that it is not always possible to keep all data. Already during the pre-processing stage a selection must be made what data is kept and which is discarded. Both in the astrophysics and cyber security cases this plays an important role and care must be taken that crucial data is not lost by accident. For the Kepler satellite mission the limited amount of bandwidth allows only 6% of the total information to be send to Earth, while the remainder is lost during the pre-processing on board the satellite. In the cyber security case, already during the pre-processing phase a selection is made which data will not be of interest for network forensics. Since majority of the network traffic is benign (e.g. web searches, visits to popular websites, social media, etc.), this can be excluded from the mining process. However, a good balance between the data that can be excluded and needs to be included requires continuous consideration.

A second consideration for dynamic data is changes that occur in the way the data is recorded. Changes can occur 'suddenly' or slowly over time, but both need to taken into account to make sure that the results obtained from mining the data stays comparable. For example, in the astronomy case, the sensors (i.e. pixels) are continuously degrading over time due to the hostile space environment, and needs to be corrected for. An example of change in the criminal justice case is the phasing out of an old database system and the introduction of a new one. Since the criminal justice chain consists of many organizations with their own database system (see Fig. 2), it is likely that at any time one is being replaced. Such a replacement always come with a revised set of attributes and corresponding definitions, and care need to be taken that the new database still allows the mining question to be answered.

The final consideration discussed is the evolution of attributes. For all kinds of reasons the original meaning of an attribute can change. Not taking into account these changes will distort the results obtained from the mining and make a comparison with previous periods difficult. Some examples are the legal reform (i.e. changing of laws) or the introduction of new penalties in the legal justice chain. When a law changes, one compares (slightly) different types of crime when looking at the periods before and after the change, while a change in penalty (e.g. from detention into a fine) could lead to a different path through the chain that has a different elapsed time. Examples from the cyber security case is the introduction of new software/hardware or changes in internet habits of the users. if these completely benign changes are not incorporated during the pre-processing phase it will increase the amount of 'non-interesting' information for network forensics or pollute the pre-processing with benign processes that do not occur anymore.

7. Conclusions

The three cases presented all show that domain knowledge plays an important role during the first two stages of the mining process. During the first stage, developing and understanding the application domain, it is no surprise that domain knowledge plays an important role, but the presented cases have shown that domain knowledge also plays a key role during the pre-processing stage. Although there are some universal guidelines on the different steps taken during the pre-processing stage, the emphasis given to each step and specific pitfalls to avoid depend on the domain. Therefore, relying only on generic rules, without taking the specific details of the domain into account, will lead to results that are difficult to interpret or could even be wrong.

Two trends can be distinguished to help determine which aspect of the pre-processing stage must be emphasized. The first trend is the consistency of the time series data. Ranging from time series data that are automatically filled by specialized sensors where the emphasis is on the noise characteristics to ones that are mainly filled by hand and have to deal with the trustworthiness of each value. The second trend that can be distinguished is the optimization of the set of records included in the time series data versus the optimization of the approach taken to answer the mining question. At one extreme the questions revolve around determining the most suitable candidates to include, while at the other extreme the questions revolve around the most suited approach.

Both trends appear to align, which suggest that they are in some way related. Looking at the overlap at the two extremes of the trends, such a relation is understandable. When there are existing data streams that were not created to answer mining question, most of the effort during the pre-processing stage will go into understanding the trustworthiness of resources at hand and determining how they can contribute in answering the mining question. Although this does require domain knowledge, the main focus will be on the combining of different data streams and resolving inconsistencies. The other extreme suggests that for time series data that are created for a specific mining purpose the noise characteristics of the candidates that will populate the time series data play an important role during the selection. This alignment can be understood when realizing that the time and money needed to invest in such very specific and dedicated mining expeditions is only obtained when previous experiments (that most likely had broader mining questions in the same specialized field) have already hinted that a more sensitive/specialized set-up will be successful. The main reason that the previous experiments could not give an unambiguous answer is most likely due to the noise characteristics that dominated the result. Getting the noise characteristics down becomes the most challenging aspect for a 'follow-up' experiment. Understanding the noise characteristics of this new experiment requires in general highly specialized knowledge, which again depends completely on the domain knowledge.

The dependence on domain knowledge is even more pronounced in the case of dynamic or time dependent data. Since most of the time too much data is collected to keep everything for the mining stage, the decision what is kept and which data to discard (permanently) must already be made during the pre-processing phase. Without a good understanding of the domain such a decision is not possible, and the possibility that crucial information is discarded increases. Furthermore, even if it is possible to store all data, domain knowledge is still necessary to guard against the evolution of the attributes or the data. Therefore, relying on some universal pre-processing tools is best avoided.

References

1. https://www-01.ibm.com/software/data/bigdata/what-is-big-data.html (last consulted October 2016.).
2. https://github.com/theodi/data-definitions (last consulted October 2016.).
3. Laney, D., 2001, '3D Data Management: Controlling Data Volume, Velocity and Variety', Gartner.
4. Vikram Phaneendra, S., and Madhusudhan Reddy, E., 2013, 'Big Data- solutions for RDBMS problems- A survey', IEEE/IFIP Network Operations & Management Symposium (NOMS 2010),Osaka Japan, Apr 19-23.
5. Jaseena, K.U., and Julie, M.D., 2014, 'Issues, Challenges and Solutions: Big Data Mining', Computer Science & Information Technology (CS & IT) 2014, pp 131-140.
6. Hulme, T., 2012, 'Understanding big data', (last consulted March 2017) https://tonyhulme.wordpress.com/2012/01/06/understanding-big-data/.
7. Thabet, N., and Soomro, T.R., 2015, 'Big Data Challenges', Computer Eng Inf Technol 2015, 4, 3.
8. Choenni, S., van Dijk, J., Leeuw, F., 2010, "Preserving privacy whilst integrating data: Applied to criminal justice." Information Polity 15.1, 2: 125-138.
9. Bargh, M.S., and Choenni, S., 2013, "On preserving privacy whilst integrating data in connected information systems", Proceedings of the International Conference on Cloud Security Management (ICCSM'13).
10. Beyer, M.A., and Laney, D., 2012, 'The importance of big data: A definition', Stamford, CT: Gartner.
11. Mell, P., and Grance, T., 2011, 'The NIST Definition of Cloud Computing', NIST Special Publication (NIST SP), 800-145.
12. Gama, J., Zliobaite, I, Bifet, A., Pechenizkiy, M., Bouchachia, A., 2014, A Survey on concept drift adaption, ACM Computing Surveys, 46(4).
13. Aigner, W., Miksch, S., Schumann, H., Tominski, C., 2011, 'Visualization of Time-Oriented Data', Springer, 2011.

14. Fayyad, U.M., Piatetsky-Shapiro, G., Smyth, P., 1996, 'From data mining to knowledge discovery in databases', AI Magazine 17(3), 37.
15. Chapman, P., Clinton, J., Kerber, R., Khabaza, T., *et al.*, 2000, 'CRIPS-DM 1.0: step-by-step data mining guide'.
16. Rohanizadeh, S.S., and Moghadam, M. B., 2009, 'A Proposed Data Mining Methodology and its Application to Industrial Procedures', Journal of Industrial Engineering, 4, pp 37-50.
17. Choenni, S., *et al.*, 2005, "Supporting technologies for knowledge management." Knowledge Management and Management Learning. Springer US, 89-112.
18. Aggarwal, C.C., 2015, 'Data Mining', Springer, pp. 457-491.
19. Kalidien, S., Choenni, S., Meijer, R., 2010, "Crime statistics online: potentials and challenges." Proceedings of the 11th Annual International Digital Government Research Conference on Public Administration Online: Challenges and Opportunities. Digital Government Society of North America.
20. van den Braak, S., Choenni, S., Verwer, S., 2013, "Combining and analyzing judicial databases", Discrimination and Privacy in the Information Society, Springer Berlin Heidelberg, 191-206.
21. Verwer, S., van den Braak, S., Choenni, S., 2013, "Sharing confidential data for algorithm development by multiple imputation", Proceedings of the 25th International Conference on Scientific and Statistical Database Management, ACM.
22. Borucki, W.J., 2016, 'KEPLER Mission: development and overview' in 'Reports on Progress in Physics', Volume 79, Issue 3.
23. Borucki, W.J., Koch, D., Basri, G., Batalha, N., Brown, T., Caldwell, D., *et al.*, 2008, 'Finding Earth-size planets in the habitable zone: the Kepler Mission', Proceedings of the International Astronomical Union, IAU Symposium, Volume 249, pp. 17-24.
24. Koch, D. G., Borucki, W. J., Basri, G., Batalha, N. M., Brown, T. M., Caldwell, D., *et al.*, 2010, 'Kepler Mission Design, Realized Photometric Performance, and Early Science', Astrophysical Journal, 713, L79.
25. Netten, N., *et al.*, 2014, "Elapsed times in criminal justice systems", Proceedings of the 8th International Conference on Theory and Practice of Electronic Governance, ACM.
26. van Dijk, J., Kalidien, S., Choenni, S., 2016, "Smart monitoring of the criminal justice system." Government Information Quarterly.
27. Pilli, E.S., Joshi, R.C., Niyogi, R., 2010, 'Network forensic frameworks: Survey and research challenges', Digital Investigation, vol. 7, no. (1-2), pp. 14-27.
28. Kerr, D.R., and Bruins, B.L., 2001, 'Network flow switching and flow data export', US Patent Number 6243667.
29. Li, B., Springer, J., Bebis, G., Hadi Gunes, M., 2013, 'A survey of network flow applications', Journal of Network and Computer Apps., 36, 567–581.
30. Cornelisse, R., Bargh, M.S., Choenni, S., Moolenaar, D.E.G., de Zeeuw, L., 2016, 'Compressing Large Amounts of NetFlow Data Using a Pattern Classification Scheme ', 2016 IEEE 2nd International Conference on Intelligent Data and Security, pp. 364-370.

Chapter 7

Data Analytics: Industrial Perspective & Solutions for Streaming Data

Mohsin Munir*, Sebastian Baumbach†, Ying Gu‡, Andreas Dengel§ and Sheraz Ahmed¶

*German Research Center for Artificial Intelligence (DFKI),
Kaiserslautern, Germany*
*mohsin.munir@dfki.de
†sebastian.baumbach@dfki.de
‡Ying.gu@dfki.de
§andreas.dengel@dfki.de
¶sheraz.ahmed@dfki.de

Over the past few years, a lot of devices and machines around us are becoming 'smart'. Based on the idea of the Internet of Things (IoT), different devices and machines can connect to the internet and communicate with each other. Such internet enabled devices are continuously observing their environment and logging a lot of data in the back-end database. By applying data analytics on the gathered Big Data, smart decisions are made to facilitate the end user according to the current situation. This capability of adaptive decision making actually makes ordinary devices and machines 'smart'. These devices and machines are becoming intelligent by learning about their surroundings from different sources, and develop the ability to avoid unforeseen situations by analyzing that data. In this chapter, we provide a comprehensive overview of how different industrial players are using data analytics to provide better services to their customers and improve their internal processes and workflows. We discuss how different industries use data analytics to gain vital insights for providing better healthcare to public, making homes more secure, increasing crop yield, delivering goods more quickly, reducing the downtime of a machine, avoiding a disease, etc. An overview of different analytics platforms and solutions used in different industries for time series and streaming data are also discussed in this chapter.

1. Introduction

We live in an age where data is becoming a key for success in every field of life. Due to rapid advancements in technology, different players in academics, research, and industry are collecting different types of data, which serve as their driving force. However, the data itself has no meaning until it is carefully analyzed. Data analytics[a] is a process of analyzing data in order to discover hidden patterns, knowledge, or trends. Many companies are using data analytics widely to add value to their business by analyzing past and current data. The process of data analytics not only includes analysis of the data, but it refers to a complete workflow which starts with data collection and other steps including data cleaning, data preparation, data governance, data analysis/modeling, and finally data visualization. Each of the steps in this workflow is a key for good analytics.

To maximize the output, efficiency, and for added value, there are different data providers, which take care of the initial steps (i.e., data cleaning, preparation, and governance) in the workflow of data analytics by providing data externally. This means that in combination with the in-house data collected by companies, there are many external data sources, which are being utilized to perform data analytics. Furthermore, due to the evolution of technology, the mode of data collection has also evolved. Especially, with the emergence of IoT, which refers to the network of physical devices, vehicles, buildings, and other items embedded with electronics, software, sensors, actuators, and network connectivity that enable these objects to collect and exchange data [1]. Recent studies show that the IoT market is growing and will continue to grow a lot over the next four years. It is expected that a market value of nearly $122 billion will be reached by the year 2022 [2]. Due to these IoT enabled devices, companies are now continuously getting live streams of huge amounts of data. This data is usually collected over a continuous interval of time, which results in time-series data. This IoT based time-series data resulted into the evolution of data analytics where in contrast to traditional data analytics where data cleaning, and analysis were at the core, now it becomes even more difficult to store and maintain the data, which is being collected by these IoT devices.

With the help of data analytics on streaming/time-series data, companies can keep an eye on different aspects, e.g., reducing maintenance costs, avoiding equipment failures, and improving business operations. In

---

[a]Data analytics and Data mining are used interchangeably nowadays. In this chapter, the term, data analytics is used. In an industrial perspective, data analytics is considered as a complete workflow, which incorporates data mining among other things.

addition, retailers, restaurant chains and makers of consumer goods can use the data from smartphones, wearable technologies, and in-home devices to do targeted marketing and promotions – the business side of the IoT's futuristic world of connected consumer gear.

Almost every industrial sector, be it health care, agriculture, manufacturing, agriculture, dairy farming, logistics, automotive, etc. is now redefining their products and enabling them to IoT for gaining maximum benefits. In this way, different industrial solutions are also available focusing specifically on data analytics on time-series data. This chapter focuses of providing insight on the different data analytics solutions available in different industrial sectors.

2. Data Analytics in Agriculture

With the increase of the world population and the improvement of living standards, the demand of high quality food is increasing. Agricultural mechanization is playing a vital role to fulfill this need with the help of large-scale production. However, the physical performance of mechanization and mass production is limited with the advancements in the fields of IoT and cloud computing, the devices for data collection and data storage have become affordable and prevalent. In the agriculture sector, data analytics can be applied on the machinery and farming data collected in order to reduce loss, improve efficiency, and lower costs under the condition of unchanged physical properties. This enables a modern farming concept called precision agriculture (PA) or satellite farming. This kind of farming helps the farmer to recognize the variations in the farming land and how to adjust input for different parts of land to optimize the output. A global positioning system (GPS) is the backbone of PA. With the help of GPS, a farmer can identify the exact area where soil conditions vary. In conjunction with the precise location, different measures like air quality, moisture level, field terrain, crop yield, crop maturity, and gas levels are recorded and turned into meaningful information using data analytics.

Data driven decision-making has been extended from the business sector to the agricultural sector. Many large enterprises in the agribusiness are becoming involved in data analytics research and development. They are providing solutions for PA and for a variety of other issues in agriculture. Fierce competition between companies has already begun.

John Deere converted their equipment to the paradigm of IoT to help farmers manage their fleet, reduce down time, and the cost of production. This information is combined with the local weather data, soil data, crop characteristics, and other data sets from different sources. **MyJohn-Deere.com** is a platform for data analytics, which provides the possibility to store, analyze, and visualize results on a web-portal (as well as on mobile application called **Mobile Farm Manager**). With the help of such platforms, farmers can figure out when and where to plant which kind of crops, when to plough and when to harvest, and which optimized path should be followed during the work. The right decision can help farmers to improve their efficiency. The data collected during different phases of farming are massive. To take advantage of the collected data, John Deere already steps into big data analysis for the future of farming.

IBM and **SignalDemand** have developed a data analytics system which uses predictive analytics to predict the demand and optimize the margin to meet the needs of different agribusiness companies. While large agricultural enterprises have large datasets, advanced equipment, data scientist, and domain experts at their disposal, the majority of farmers neither have access to such information nor the resources to get benefits from advancements in technology. To help farmers who are working on a small-scale and lack the technology infrastructure, IBM built a back-office network. They supply corn-specific information on a regular basis, along with generalized information on fertilizer and weather conditions to registered farmers via their mobile phones. A farmer can get timely agronomic intelligence simply via automated voice mail or text messages on his mobile phone.

aWhere (an American corporation) collects and analyzes over a billion points of data (which is a pivot element for analysis) from around the globe each day to create unprecedented visibility and insight which is known as Agricultural Intelligence. This intelligence is used for critical decision making from farm level through to national policy [3]. High-quality weather data is combined and analyzed purely for agricultural use. Their major data analytics solutions are **Weather Terrain, Weather Agronomics,** and **Weather Support**.

The Climate Corporation (a San Francisco-based company) examines weather data to provide insurance to farmers who can lock in profits even in the case of drought, heavy rains, or other adverse weather conditions. **FieldView** is their data analytics solution, which combines farmers' field data with real-time and past – soil, crop, and weather data to help them efficiently manage their operations and gain insights into their fields [4]. In addition to the FieldView, they also provide a hardware solution **SeedSense** for Planter Monitoring. Perfect planter performance can be achieved by maximizing planter speed and adjusting vacuum pressure by using SeenSense. It also enables the farmer to sow precisely, maintain depth, avoid compaction, and troubleshoot mechanical problems.

The CropOS is a data analytics platform, which uses machine learning and cloud biology to improve crop performance and help scientists and breeders with some of the biggest challenges in the agriculture sector. It is developed and maintained by Benson Hill Biosystems, which is an agricultural solutions company. They unlock the global genetic potential of plants to enhance the sustainability of food, feed, fiber, and fuel production [5]. CropOS represents a uniquely powerful platform at the intersection of big data, machine learning, and plant biology. CropOS empowers researchers to significantly increase the yield of major food crops and identify the most promising plant genetics in weeks instead of studying long growing seasons.

CLAAS focuses very much on self-propelled machines developing and producing combine harvesters, self-propelled forage harvesters and tractors [6]. Self-propelled machines are very important especially for crops like wheat, rye, barley, and corn, which have to be harvested at just the right point of maturity. Once this harvest maturity has been reached, the combine harvesters work in the fields day and night. In this process, up to 50 parameters from the reel to the chopper influence the harvest yield. The operator has to continuously monitor and evaluate around a dozen of these parameters. Hardly any operator is capable of keeping an eye on everything and tapping the machine's full potential. To solve this problem, CLAAS also moved toward IoT enabled combine harvesters. In addition to this, an assistance and analytics system is used, which permanently monitors the harvesting process and automatically adjusts the machine setting to the current conditions which is faster and more precise when compared to a human operator. Furthermore, together with the German Research Center for Artificial Intelligence (DFKI), and the Fraunhofer Institute of Optronics, System Technologies, and Image Exploitation (IOSB), CLASS is working on extending the data analytics to improve the performance of mobile work machines with unsupervised anomaly detection algorithms, which can detect unexpected events without any previous domain knowledge.

3. Data Analytics in Healthcare

Similar to agriculture, data analytics is playing a vital role in the advancement of the healthcare sector. With the easy availability of smart devices (including smart watches, smart phones, and smart wristbands), a new dimension of healthcare has emerged – Smart Healthcare. The end-user smart devices are continuously collecting users' data regarding different activities performed over a day, month, or year using different sensors.

Data analytics on smart sensors' data have opened new dimensions of research and applications in Connected or Smart healthcare. Smart healthcare is supporting, and slowly replacing traditional healthcare. By analyzing the streaming data generated by smart wearables, it is possible to see if a user is healthy, or if some preventive measures are required, in order to avoid a potential health problem. Now doctors can remotely examine their patients and suggest treatments on the go. Smart healthcare offers many new possibilities for patients too. Patients can keep updated with their health and fitness data all the time, find other patients suffering with the same disease to discuss various treatments, and easily track the post-surgical needs. The digitization of patient health data encourages the communication and collaboration of all the stakeholders involved in the patient's health. For instance, i) government institutes can use the data to extract different statistics and to make policies as needed, ii) pharmaceutical companies can use the data to track the positive or negative effects of different medicines, iii) doctors can use this data to choose a treatment when a patient has high cardiovascular risk, etc. With smart and connected healthcare, healthcare is shifting from being episodic/reactive to preventive/proactive. Different companies (mentioned below) are providing solutions for connected, smart, or preventive healthcare.

IBM Healthcare is a data analytics solution, which focuses on health monitoring and intervention, analyzing streaming data (such as data generated in ICU), and helping in detecting signs of various changes occurring in a patient's health. The detected early signs are used to generate medical alerts for proactive intervention. It also enables healthcare providers to improve operational performance, reduce cost of care, and counter fraud in healthcare by using integrated data management and analytics. Furthermore, it provides consumer level analytics to understand consumer preferences and behaviors by capturing data from different sources such as claims, clinical history, and social platforms; and then merges all the data into one unified view. It also helps building a predictive model that evaluates the risk of readmission for patients with chronic obstructive pulmonary disease [7]. Researchers at National Institutes of Health (NIH) are using **IBM PureData** System for analytics to unlock new insights from data gathered over decades. With the help of this system, researchers can run analysis on large, complex data sets (both clinical and genomic research data) and generate reports faster than ever before [8].

SAP Real-Time Analytics is a complete solution for patient care, human resources, finance, care collaboration, and healthcare analytics. The big health data collected from electronic health records, research, physician notes, insurance claims, and social media data are used by SAP Real-Time Analytics to reduce cost and improve quality of care. This solution enables data scientists to separate noise from signals and derive meaningful insights from the data. The unified analytics model transform data from a wide range of sources into actionable information. Seoul National University Bundang Hospital (South Korea) has developed its clinical data warehouse (CDW) using **SAP Data Services** and **SAP HANA**. Their CDW is used to automate the clinical indicators system, gather critical data in real-time, provide instantaneous feedback to clinicians, and provide multidimensional analyses based on patient characteristics, diseases, and location [9].

General Electric (GE) provides many healthcare solutions in general; and some solutions are based on data analytics in the areas of diagnosis, clinical decision-making, and asset monitoring. The GE **Marquette 12SL ECG** analysis program provides diagnostic confidence to care providers by giving fast and reliable cardiac care decisions. In the area of patient monitoring, GE provides **CARESCAPE Central Station** which allows the integration of different medical devices and systems to access patient's historical data. When a patient moves to a care area, this solution enables care providers to perform in-depth analyses and offers clinical decision support. **Centricity Imaging Analytics** is a real-time dashboard which provides visibility into the workflows of the radiology department for increasing department throughput and patient care.

Combined Applications to Reduce Exposure (CARE) (by Siemens) is an analytics solution, which is designed to improve dose monitoring in different interventional radiology systems. The dose of an individual patient is recorded in addition to other data, such as CT-dose index, dose length product, and total recording time. This data is also used to enhance dose reporting and assessment, transparency regarding dose per case, reporting on patient dose history, and cross-institutional reporting.

Apple CareKit is an open source platform for creating health related apps to regularly track care plans, monitor users' progress, and share their insights. *One Drop* (by Informed Data Systems, Inc.) is an example of such a mobile app created using CareKit. **Apple ResearchKit** enables developers to create apps, which enable researchers and doctors to gather robust and meaningful data for their health related studies, and obtain a complete history of their patients. The real life data collected is used to find physical patterns, correlation between physical history and medication, predict a particular problem, and recommend diet and fitness plans. With the help of ResearchKit and CareKit, researchers use Apple Watch to predict seizures before they actually happen. For instance, *EpiWatch* (an Apple Watch app by Johns Hopkins University) enables people to accurately track the onset and duration of seizures in real time. A patient sensing an impending seizure launches the app on Apple Watch and an alert is automatically sent to a designated family member or caregiver. Similarly, *Asthma Health* (by Weill Medical College), *Concussion Tracker* (by NYU Langone Medical Center), *GlucoSuccess* (by Massachusetts General Hospital), and *C Tracker* (by Boston Children's Hospital) are examples of such apps which are built on top of CareKit and ResearchKit.

4. Data Analytics in Manufacturing

Data analytics provides a granular approach to diagnose and improve whole manufacturing flaws. It is always in the manufacturers' interest to improve their production processes, product quality, production cycle, and the amount of output per unit of input. Due to the involvement of a number of players and processes in the manufacturing life cycle, it is hard to find the cause of failure or inefficiency exactly. With the growth of Industrial IoT in recent years, everything is going digital and connected. With the help of this digitization and connectivity, a lot of streaming data related to equipment, automation, production lines, systems, and products are generated and stored. Manufacturers can use data analytics to leverage the data collected from on-the-floor factory machinery alongside other traditional (factory logs) and social data. Some of the advantages of using data analytics in manufacturing are to – i) get unexpected insights into different processes, ii) increase accuracy, quality, and yield (amount of output per unit of input), iii) improve the forecast of product supply and demand, iv) enhance the understanding of plant performance across multiple metrics, v) boost the product quality, vi) track all products with defected components, vii) predict machine failure, viii) quantify how daily production impacts financial performance, ix) provide preemptive maintenance and service by continuously monitoring a product instead of fixed term maintenance, and x) identify the root cause of a failure. Figure 1 shows how advance data analytics can help decode and improve complex manufacturing processes.

The main challenges in manufacturing are a lack of collaboration across different departments, disparate systems and data sources, and difficulty in coordinating supply and demand chains. Such challenges, among others

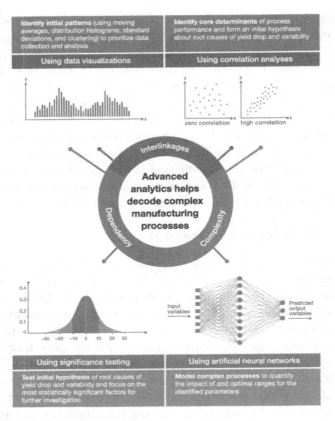

Fig. 1.   This figure shows how advanced analytics can be used in streamlining manufacturing value chains by finding the core determinants of process performance [10].

are tackled in the solutions provided by different companies using advanced
data analytics.

IBM Analytics provides a complete analytics solution to be used in automotive, defense, chemical, petroleum, energy, aerospace, electronics, and
other industries to uncover deeper insights into operations, inventory, market demands, supply chain, and performance [11]. By applying advanced
data analytics on aggregated data from different sources (such as different
sensors, maintenance logs, and production systems), manufacturers can efficiently achieve their demand, production, and supply requirements; while
properly managing all the resources at minimal cost. It can integrate structured as well as unstructured data from different sources. IBM analytics can
unveil a number of critical manufacturers questions, such as how operating

costs can be reduced while having better project financial performance, how greater visibility into supply chains can be achieved, how the supply chain's needs can be predicted, and how the maintenance cost can be cut down. It can also uncover insights into customers' behavior, their needs, and market trends to make better business decisions. Nowadays, production assets and consumer products are transmitting vital operational data to backend data warehouses. **IBM Predictive Maintenance and Quality** software solution leverages the data collected from different sources and predicts when a particular asset or machine needs maintenance. In contrast to the traditional scheduled maintenance, predictive maintenance recommends when maintenance is required and when it is not. This type of maintenance helps to keep critical production lines and consumer products running, while saving money and minimizing customer inconvenience. Muller, Inc., USA, is a retailer and manufacturer of metal products. They used *IBM Cognos Business Intelligence, IBM Cognos TM1, IBM SPSS Modeler, and IBM Business Analytics* to pull data from all points of sale, inventory, and ERP systems; so that the employees can view and analyze company data, measure individual performance, and access how their work affects the bottom line [12]. The Vaasan group (a leading bakery operator in Northern Europe) used IBM Analytics to enhance forecasting and inventory management. The solution based on the *IBM Cognos Controller, IBM Cognos Intelligence, and IBM Cognos 8 Planning* enabled the bakery to predict production requirements and helped them prepare for fluctuating orders [13].

SAP provides multiple solutions in the domain of manufacturing. SAP **Manufacturing Execution System** connects, monitors, and controls different manufacturing operations. With the help of automated data collection, it provides visibility into the manufacturing processes which helps process managers to find and resolve quality issues. Its asset utilization functionality improves overall equipment effectiveness, facilitates predictive maintenance, and minimizes downtime. SAP **Enterprise Resource Planning (ERP)** is an enterprise level system for streamlining the manufacturing, services, sales, finances, and human resource processes. It is composed of different modules, which accelerate the entire manufacturing process, boost sales and customer satisfaction, provide support for administration tasks, streamline and automate financial operations, and provides real-time analytics based on ERP data. SAP **Manufacturing Integration and Intelligence (MII)** is the solution for smart manufacturing which exploit the data collected from Industrial Internet of Things (IIoT).

It automates the IIoT and facilitates in manufacturing data transformation and integration. This software is equipped with the **Manufacturing Analytics Platform**, which provides statistical process control and predictive analytics. It can also identify the root cause of machine downtime and efficiency loss; which makes the maintenance task easy for technicians and helps the operation team to improve efficiency. The SAP **Predictive Maintenance and Service** solution leverages the IoT data to transform reactive maintenance to predictive maintenance. It provides the visibility into manufacturing asset and consumer product health by remotely observing their behavior and patterns. By analyzing the Big Data collected, future needs are predicted [14].

Microsoft Azure IoT is a complete suite for connecting IoT devices, collecting IoT data, analyzing the collected data, and mining disparate data [15]. Existing data and systems can also be integrated with new data sources to create new insights and business models. A Predictive Analytics module in Azure provides insight into how a certain product behaves in normal conditions and in other special conditions by finding patterns and correlations in historical and new sensor data. Based on such analytics, this suite is able to provide warning signs, identify where a problem exists, and notify when equipment needs maintenance. With such preemptive warnings, small repairs can be made before big failures occur. It also helps in prioritizing the maintenance task by providing information about which equipment is at high risk. Once an actual root cause of the failure is detected, it can facilitate a technician by recommending the error code (with possible fixes) for that condition. The technician's time of finding the root cause of a failure is saved, now he just has to fix the defective component (with the help of some recommendations about possible fixes). This suite enables manufacturers to remotely monitor their assets, which are deployed outside the factory. Automatic notifications can be triggered on this live data to get real-time asset feedback and maintenance requests.

General Electric (GE) Brilliant Manufacturing is a software suite, which connects people, machines, materials, and processes in IoT. This suite maximizes manufacturing production performance and optimizes operations through advanced real-time analytics. It allows the integration and aggregation of whole manufacturing life cycle data from the beginning till the end. Data driven analytics from disparate manufacturing sources allow manufacturers to take optimal decisions to drive improvements in end-to-end production [16]. This suite includes different products including the following: i) **Efficiency Analyzer** provides an up-to-date view of the entire production process and transforms real-time machine data into action efficiency metrics. Such unified metrics help plant managers to reduce unplanned downtime, maximize yield, improve production quality, increase flexibility, and maximize team productivity. ii) **Production Quality Analyzer** analyzes data to catch non-conforming events before they occur to help quality engineers to easily identify the problem. iii) **Production Execution Supervisor** digitizes documentation, instructions, orders, and process steps, enabling manufacturers to get the right information at the right time. iv) **Product Genealogy Manager** builds a record of all equipment, raw materials, tools, and personnel which are required to build the finished goods. It helps service personnel to manage services in an efficient way.

Manufacturing Analytics by BOSCH is a solution for analyzing production data. Different types of data such as test, process, and machine data from different sources can be used to improve the production process and product quality while reducing the cost with the help of this suite. This suite can integrate the existing production data with the new data. The predictive models can be applied to real-time data for predictive maintenance and root cause analysis. Data analytics unveils the previously unknown correlations in data and helps manufacturers in gaining new insights. The newly discovered data insights and prediction models can be applied using this suite to automate the analytics process.

SAS provides different solutions to get the best out of the manufacturing life cycle. SAS **Demand-Driven Planning and Optimization** suite improves the supply and demand planning processes. This suite uses analytical insights of demand patterns to help manufacturers in making supply plans, which are aligned with the demand forecast. Production and logistics can also be managed to match the ever-changing customer needs and market dynamics. SAS **Quality Analytics** suite includes data mining and predictive analytic technologies for predictive maintenance and identification of potential problems. It also helps in reducing the total cost of quality by reducing the scrap and rework, and identifying design and production defects. SAS **Field Quality Analytics** helps in making aftermarket service efficient by integrating and analyzing internal and external data sources. It helps in detecting and prioritizing warranty and service issues. SAS **Customer Intelligence 360** collects, analyzes, and reports on customer experiences to improve sales and marketing performance. It provides insight into customer segmentation: which customer groups are more likely to buy which kind of product and why. With the help of such forecasts, advertising and promotion campaigns can be planned and targeted at customer groups [17].

5. Data Analytics in Connected Vehicles

A connected vehicle is a vehicle designed with the capability of connecting to the internet and other connected devices including smart phones, traffic lights, other vehicles on the road, smart home appliances, etc. It is predicted by Gartner, Inc. that by the year 2020, one in five vehicles in the world will have some form of wireless connectivity in them, which adds up to 250 million connected vehicles [18]. The accumulated data based on driver's behavior, car machinery, sensors installed in the car and in the surroundings can leverage data analytics in the following functional areas: autonomous driving, safety, infotainment, well-being of driver's health, vehicle management, mobility management, and smart home integration [19]. Vehicle manufactures like BMW and Volkswagen are making these connected vehicles smart by introducing functionalities like autonomous car parking and emergency assist respectively. Data analytics provides car manufacturers with crucial insights into the vehicle system, behavior of the vehicles in certain conditions, and drivers' patterns. Thousands of components inside the vehicle are continuously logging data. Even if the test driver observes an unexpected shifting characteristic, it is hard for a manufacturer to exactly find the defective component or the contributing components. But, with the help of data analytics, the defective component and the contributing components can be figured out precisely.

Ford and **IBM** are working together to develop a platform which analyzes data collected from a vehicle. Based on the small chunks of vehicular data, this platform can spot patterns, correlations, and trends to help the driver make efficient transportation decisions. Data collected from Ford **Smart Mobility Experimentation Platform** helps their scientists to spot tendencies and behaviors, and their customers to have a better travel experience. They are working on using real-time analytics to learn about a problem on a particular route by taking data feed from different systems [20]. In the domain of predictive maintenance, Ford is working on sending personalized oil change and brake maintenance notifications to drivers. The collected data is statistically analyzed in order to evaluate the maintenance needs for each vehicle separately [21].

Daimler is making their cars and trucks intelligent by enabling them with anticipatory planning. Based on data from different sources, their vehicles are able to operate on an anticipatory basis in which they can foresee different things which the human eye cannot see. Their trucks and buses are equipped with **Predictive Powertrain Control** (PPC), which can anticipate the terrain and adjust the vehicle accordingly. Based on the 3D map data, PPC adjusts the vehicle speed and gear selection optimally to the topography of the transport route. This control reduces fuel consumption by up to 5% [22].

BMW group is also using **IBM Big Data and Analytics** technology to optimize their products, repairs, and maintenance processes. **IBM SPSS** predictive analytics software is used to combine and analyze data from different sources like pre-production sensor data, workshop notes, and numerous test drives of prototypes [23]. In this way, different vulnerabilities can be identified quickly, and eliminated before the model goes into series production. Before this automated process, this evaluation took months to complete. IBM Big Data and Analytics are used to analyze data from all available sources to discover anomalous patterns and predict maintenance needs.

Volkswagen, in collaboration with CSC (a technology solutions and service provider company), use data analytics to support predictive marketing to increase aftermarket service revenues [24]. They combine customer data with vehicle data, and notes written by technicians at the service centers. With the help of that data, they are able to predict upcoming maintenance for specific drivers.

Tesla car manufacturer is collecting data from their connected cars and using telematics to batch stream key data points to backend big data pool. The collected data enable engineers and manufacturing lines to resolve the issues and send back fixes with their over-the-air software updates. They are providing continuously improving customer experience based on the data and analytic views [25].

Audi is also making its vehicles intelligent with a vision to reduce fuel consumption. The predictive efficiency assistant enables the vehicle to slow down or automatically adjust the speed to the conditions in an anticipatory manner. The system analyzes the route topography, speed limits, road users ahead, and navigation data.

Caterpillar, Inc. is the world's leading manufacturer of construction and mining equipment. They have created a new organizational division called Analytics and Innovation (AI) to form a broad and connected analytics ecosystem. The data collected from gigantic machines are used to develop predictive and proscriptive information. This predictive diagnostics is shifting their customers from reactive (repair after failure) to proactive (repair before failure) mode [26]. By using data analytics, they are able to point out inefficiencies in the operation of a particular machine by comparing its operational data with that machine's benchmark data.

6. Data Analytics in Logistics

Logistics service providers move masses of goods from one location to another. A lot of data related to shipments, origin, destination, size, weight, and content are stored per shipment. Some of the advantages of using data analytics in the logistics sector are, i) optimization of delivery time, resource utilization, and geographical coverage, ii) goods storage capacity and required resources forecast, iii) valuable insight into customer sentiment and product quality, and iv) insight into the global flow of goods.

DHL uses big data analytics to make their operations more efficient. Rapid processing of real-time information enables their **SmartTruck** to optimize the delivery route in real-time. Delivery routes are also automatically updated according to traffic conditions. Unsuccessful delivery attempts are avoided in intelligent routing, based on the availability and location information provided by the recipient. SmartTrucks are re-routed on the go, based on the combined analytics of geographical factors, environmental factors, and recipient data [27]. It is important for a logistics company to plan operational capacity in time. The optimal planning cannot be done by neglecting external factors, such as unexpected bankruptcy, a regional outbreak disease, or natural disasters etc. DHL Solutions and Innovation is working on an analytics tool to measure external factors on the expected volume of shipment to make efficient shipment volume prediction. Based on the shipment records, DHL provides an online geo marketing tool **Geovista**, to analyze business potential. This tool provides a sales forecast and local competitor analysis. DHL is also working on a Supply Chain Risk Management Solution which will improve the resilience of logistic providers entire supply chain with the help of predictive analytics on a global scale (by aggregating data from different local sources such as politics, economy, nature, health, etc.).

Amazon was the first company to give recommendations about items in which a user might be interested. Today, it uses different parameters (such as, which items are bought by a particular user before, what he has in his wish list and virtual cart, which items he has rated or viewed, and which items a similar user has bought) to customize the browsing and buying experience. Predictive analytics is used to ensure the right item must be in stock when a customer orders it. Amazon is taking data analytics to a different level with its patent on *Anticipatory Shipping*. The patent is officially called 'Method and system for anticipatory package shipping'. The idea of anticipatory shipping is to predict who will order what and when, and then ship that item even before it is ordered. Another scenario is also discussed in patent for 'speculative shipping'. In this type of shipping, a package is sent to a geographical area, without completely specifying the delivery address at the time of shipment - the package might remain in near continuous transit on trucks until a customer makes a purchase [28]. In this way, the package is shipped to the customer instantaneously.

7. Data Analytics in Dairy Market

The current trend of automation and data exchange in modern manufacturing is inextricably linked with the production industry as it helps making cars autonomous or factories more productive. Nowadays, not only these industries can benefit from IoT, but one of the oldest sector of mankind, i.e., milk production, is also taking advantage of smart technologies. For a long time, the dairy market has been suffering from low prices, which means that modern technologies and data analytics can neither influence market prices, nor the bargaining power of the dairy, nor the retail industry. However, these new technological trends can help farmers to reduce their production costs and enable them to produce more milk by keeping a keen eye on their cows health.

Effects of the globalized milk market are already noticeable. Farmers are suffering mostly from the extremely sharp fall in prices. The low milk prices make it nearly impossible for farmers to obtain profits, as they are not covering costs. They are forced to optimize their production. Legal requirements and a change in social perception restricted many alternatives, like the prophylactic use of antibiotics in Europe, for optimization [29]. The only chance to raise their economic performance is to reduce costs and increase the efficiency of their production.

The welfare of cows is of enormous importance for farmers because only healthy and happy cows give the maximum amount of milk. The farmers are able to determine the health of their cows themselves, but this is only true for small herd sizes. Farmers lack the time to monitor each cow individually in herds of dozens or hundreds of cows as can be found nowadays [30]. This is why farmers are making more frequent use of tracking systems and data analytics for the automatic health monitoring of their herd.

These tracking systems take advantage of the architecture of modern barns in Central Europe and North America, in which cows can move around freely. As a result, the everyday movement and activity behavior of cows is an important indicator of their health and whether they are in heat. In general, sick cows move less than cows without any diseases as shown in Figure 2. When cows are in heat, they move much more. The movement behavior is commonly measured with either accelerometers or pedometers embedded into the collar of each cow. These sensors are the central component in these systems as they are measuring the activity and vital parameters of the equipped cows continuously and autonomously.

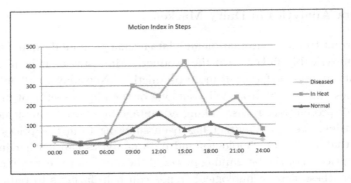

Fig. 2. Simplified movement behavior of cows. Different conditions of cows can be classified based on their movement patterns.

In more recent times, acceleration sensors are used instead of pedometers. They are superior since they cannot only recognize the amount of activity, but also the precise type of movement: walking, running, or lying. From a data perspective, the sensors are just counting steps, which do not tell the farmer anything directly about the health of a cow. However, the number of steps per day is a strong indicator, and it is directly linked to diseases and in heat detection of individual cows in the herd. The smart dairy products are sold by *SCR Europe, Lely, DairyMaster,* and *DeLaval.* They have all placed sensors in the collars of cows and the data is transferred wirelessly to the server station (in most cases, by using proprietary radio standards). By analyzing that data, data analytics provide meaningful information about the cow's health and notify when it is in heat. SCR Europe product named **Heatime** and Lely product named **Qwes-H** also integrate rumination detection. It tells the farmer how much time each cow spends on ruminating which is an essential indicator for their health and whether they are in heat if the average time per day differs significantly [31].

In the year 2014, the first tracking system based on locating cows within the barns entered the market. **Smartbow** and **CowView** draw the diagnosis from positioning data of cows instead of using pedometers or accelerometers. Both systems utilize an ultra-wide band (UWB) RFID techniques in combination with an approach based on Time Difference of Arrival (TDOA) for locating the cows [32].

Indoor location techniques directly measure the distance traveled by cows instead of indirectly "guessing" them based on step counts or accelerometer values. Data analytics in this case works the same way as for the step count: under certain thresholds, which already had been figured out in studies a priori, cows are marked as in heat while they are classified as diseased above this threshold.

Beyond health monitoring, the determination of being in heat is a very sensitive process as the determination of the correct time is essential for a successful insemination. A failed insemination not only leads to repeated insemination costs, but also results in lower milk production. Nowadays, the insemination of cows in the dairy industry is done synthetically. In contrast to bulls (which can smell the hormones of cows and interpret their behavior), humans can only draw their conclusions based on the interpretation of their behavior. Studies show that the in heat observation plays a time-consuming role – three times a day, 15 minutes of observation are needed for complete heat detection (in addition to the normal working hours in the cowshed) [30]. It is understandable that the farmers need automated heat detection as an alternative to the time-consuming manual observation. The same kind of sensors as used for health monitoring can also be used for in heat detection. Cows in heat, feature a special characteristic in their movement behavior which significantly differs from healthy as well as diseased cows (see Figure 2). This movement behavior can be used to draw conclusions not only about health, but also about being in heat. The tracking systems help farmers to reduce their costs for insemination and again, increase their milk yield.

Now farmers are able to access data about the health and movement behaviors of their herd from their PC, notebook, or smartphone anywhere and at anytime. More importantly, they are notified if a cow shows an abnormal pattern like a reduced feeding behavior. These alarms enable the farmer to look after their cows and call a veterinarian if required before it is too late. Not only the welfare of cows, but also the economic performance of farmers is this improved. Sick cows cause high veterinarian and drug costs for the farmers. Tackling these issues in time also leads to a better yield due to increased milk production. As a result, modern IoT-based products as well as data analytics improve the quality of dairy products and enable farmers to spend less time in the barn.

8. Data Analytics in Smart Homes

The IT market research company, Gartner predicts that in 2022, there will be more than 500 smart objects in an average family household [33]. The smart home market is now flooded with IoT based devices. Many of the manufacturers are embedding wireless data exchange and interoperability into their devices.

Heating control is one of the areas in smart homes where people can actually save money. Products like **Thermostat+** (by ELV) and **Comet Blue** (by EUROtronic Technology) can easily be installed without even drilling a single hole [34, 35]. Heating control devices are easily plugged onto radiators, and are commonly shipped together with sensor windows (to get the knowledge if the window is close or open) and a gateway. The gateway bridges the heating control devices wirelessly so that a PC or smartphone can control the whole system. These smart devices enable customers to define the rules for temperature by the room, and to control and monitor their heating remotely from anywhere. Customers can specify the required temperature and define different time slots when they are not at home. With the help of data analytics applied on the collected data, people can analyze their habits and behaviors to save energy and more importantly for them – money.

Radio-controlled sockets are cheap and small devices which can be plugged between normal sockets and the device to be powered, such as **Parce One** [36]. They are commonly equipped with Bluetooth 4.0 alias Low Energy and are easily connectible with modern Android or iPhone based smart phones. With the help of these smart sockets, i) customers can (gain the possibility to) monitor the exact power consumption of their electronic devices and, ii) they can define rules when the device gets switched on or off. With these smart sockets, all of the electrical devices can be turned into smart devices by switching them on and off autonomously. The data of the consumed energy can be analyzed per device, which gives customers the possibility to limit the use of a particular device which helps in minimizing the overall energy consumption.

The scope of smart homes is not confined only to the inside area of a home. Gardena is regularly offering new products in order to make gardens and gardening smart [37]. **Gardena's Sensor Control Set** contains a smart gateway (which has to be installed indoors and connected via Wi-Fi or cable to the network), magnetic valves for taps, and plant sensors. The plant sensor measures temperature, soil humidity, and light intensity. These values can be used to define irrigation profiles. The goal of this application is to automatically identify if the plant needs some water or fertilizer. There is a link between the level of photosynthesis within a plant and its energy supply. Once the soil is dry, the magnetic valve is automatically opened. Customers can fine-tune the irrigation rules, for instance, based on the type of plant. Aquatic plants need more water than a cactus that will survive even if the soil is dry. Environmental factors complicate the data analytics part in this application field. However, a smart irrigation system saves a labor force and more importantly, helps plants to survive even if their owners are not present.

Now, most smart home devices are capable of measuring their surroundings, such as temperature, power consumption, or soil humidity. Additionally, they have the possibility to interact with their environment like switching off devices, activating the heating, or watering plants. What they currently lack is autonomous learning to interact with their environment based on the measured values. Nowadays, the customers still have to manually define some rules for each device. But, there are some systems which are becoming intelligent with the help of analyzing data from different sensors.

Apple wanted to change this situation with the development of **Home-Kit**: a powerful, interoperable smart home control system which is easy and fast to set up and usable on iOS devices out of the box [38]. Certified vendors and products (which are currently limited in number) can be connected to iOS over Wi-Fi or Bluetooth 4.0. Afterwards, the connected devices can be verbally configured, controlled, and monitored via Apple Siri. Besides the fact that smart home devices have to support Apple's Home-Kit and implement its functions into their system, Siri is not yet capable of communicating with people in a way one would expect or wish (to have it). For example, Siri only listens to commands containing the exact name of a device (which has to be defined a priori). General descriptions, which are often used in colloquial and everyday language, are not understood for now.

Vivint is one of the largest home automation companies in North America. Different smart home devices including small appliances, HVAC (Heating, ventilation and air conditioning), security systems, video devices, thermostats, smart doors and locks, smart bulbs, and smoke alarms are connected via Vivint touchscreen panel and make a network of smart devices. That network produces a lot of streaming data, which is stored in Hadoop – an open source framework, for processing and storage of extremely large datasets. They use Datameer (a big data analytics platform) to shorten the time of using raw data for different analytics and actionable intelligence purposes [39]. The collected data is analyzed to better understand the usage patterns of different smart devices, which can be further used to improve the service and reduce energy consumption.

Google Nest offers smart devices including security cameras, thermostats, and smoke detectors. These are devices of daily use which have been in use for ages. But, data analytics and big data have changed the way these devices work. Before becoming 'smart', these devices were used to just record videos, maintain heating to a certain level, and sound the alarm when smoke is detected, respectively. Now, by learning user behavior, Nest's smart thermostat adapts to the user's usage and season changes. It automatically controls the temperature by learning the user schedule. By detecting unwanted events inside and outside a home, and making smart alerts, **Nest Aware** software makes security cameras intelligent. In contrast to the old security cameras which only record the video, Nest's smart security cameras can make custom alerts for the activities a user is interested in. By making the smart notifications, Nest's smoke detectors can tell the user (by speaking or by making mobile notification) in which room there is smoke and gives early warnings to avoid any emergency situation. It can distinguish between steam, food burn, carbon monoxide, and smoke. These smart devices can also be connected to each other to make a home safer and more secure. For example, security cameras, light bulbs, and window shades can work together to give an impression that you are at home when you are away. Or, when a thermostat is set to 'away', it can automatically turn on the security camera. By using data analytics, such smart devices can build up a profile which allows them to intelligently adjust themselves to the environment, minimize human effort, maximize human safety, improve service quality, and save energy [40].

The smart home vision affords many business opportunities, but also faces many challenges. Currently, smart devices are hindered by a lack of interoperability and the communication standard between products designed by different manufacturers. There are different products which are trying to integrate and bridge as many different products, protocols, and wireless standards as possible. **Mediola Gateway V4+** produced by Mediola supports both 433 and 868 MHz [41]. The advantage is that various sensors and products of different manufacturers can interoperate which enable customers to mix them in rules and profiles. This works quite well; at least as long as Mediola supports them.

The smart home market is a mix of many different networking technologies and protocols, which are mostly proprietary and not designed for interoperation. All producers in the domain of smart home want a big piece of the cake to consolidate their market position. Thus, they are intending to raise barriers for new producers to enter this market by using proprietary protocols and prevent interoperability between different products. The market will most likely remain technically fragmented through 2020 [33]. From a consumer point of view, their biggest concern is data privacy. There is a need to develop a trust between the service provider and the consumer. It is very important for a consumer that the important information collected about their private life is only used to facilitate them, and not for earning money by selling that information to a third party without the consent of the consumer.

9. Conclusion

This chapter provides an insight into different industrial solutions available for data analytics. In addition to analytics on traditional data, most of these solutions are focusing on the data analytics on streaming/time-series data coming from IoT enabled devices. Almost all fields of life are benefiting from data analytics, including agriculture, healthcare, manufacturing, logistics, crowd analysis, dairy farming, smart homes, etc. This chapter attempts to provide a state-of-the-art in industrial/commercial data analytics solutions available in different fields. A deeper look at these solutions shows that there is still a lot of room and potential for improvement. Especially, most of the existing solutions are based either on traditional statistical-based approaches or to some extent using machine learning. However, almost none of the existing solutions is using the potential of deep learning, which could be very helpful to bring these analytics to the fingertips of data scientists and end users. Big players like Microsoft, Apple, SAP, and IBM have already developed cloud-based solutions, which are very suitable for streaming and time-series data. This already facilitates data scientists and companies a lot in terms of handling and managing the big streaming data from IoT devices. Companies are also making explicit efforts to evolve their analytics methods, which can deal with big data to gain maximum benefit from the collected data.

References

[1] E. Brown. Who Needs the Internet of Things? https://www.linux.com/news/who-needs-internet-things (Sept., 2016). Online; Accessed: 2017-01-01.

[2] General Electric. Smart home market. https://tinyurl.com/gr29h7v (May, 2016). Online; Accessed: 2016-12-14.

[3] J. Corbett. Localized Real-Time Agronomic Weather Data: A Big Data Foundation to Improve and Monitor Agriculture Production. http://www.awhere.com/about/news/localized-real-time-agronomic-weather-data-a%E2%80%9Dbig (June, 2016). Online; Accessed: 2017-02-02.

[4] S. Eathington. Pulling Back the Curtain on Our Innovation Pipeline. http://www.climateinsights.com/2017-innovation-pipeline/ (Jan., 2017). Online; Accessed: 2017-03-02.

[5] Benson Hill Biosystems, Inc. Benson Hill Biosystems Launches CropOS. http://bensonhillbio.com/benson-hill-biosystems-launches-cropostm/ (May, 2016). Online; Accessed: 2017-01-02.

[6] L. Henderson. CLAAS: The Harvesting Specialists. http://www.agrimarketing.com/s/38408 (Jan., 2006). Online; Accessed: 2017-01-02.

[7] IBM Corporation. PinnacleHealth System: Transforming healthcare delivery with insight into the "when" and "why" of readmissions. http://www-01.ibm.com/common/ssi/cgi-bin/ssialias?subtype=AB&infotype=PM&appname=SWGE_YT_YT_USEN&htmlfid=YTC03945USEN&attachment=YTC03945USEN.PDF (2015). Online; Accessed: 2016-06-09.

[8] IBM Corporation. National Institutes of Health: Finding cures faster by transforming big data into valuable clinical insight. http://www-01.ibm.com/common/ssi/cgi-bin/ssialias?subtype=AB&infotype=PM&htmlfid=IMC14949USEN&attachment=IMC14949USEN.PDF (July, 2015). Online; Accessed: 2016-06-09.

[9] SAP. Seoul National University Bundang Hospital: Transforming Patient Care and Data Access with SAP HANA. http://go.sap.com/documents/2015/09/d688d2a6-417c-0010-82c7-eda71af511fa.html (2015). Online; Accessed: 2016-06-15.

[10] E. Auschitzky, M. Hammer, and A. Rajagopaul. How Big Data can Improve Manufacturing. http://www.mckinsey.com/business-functions/operations/our-insights/how-big-data-can-improve-manufacturing (July, 2014). Online; Accessed: 2016-06-21.

[11] IBM Corporation. IBM Analytics. http://www.ibm.com/analytics/us/en/industry/# (2016). Online; Accessed: 2016-06-22.

[12] IBM Corporation. Using enhanced cognitive analytics to gain a competitive edge by finding valuable answers to questions not yet asked. http://presidionwp.s3-eu-west-1.amazonaws.com/wp-content/uploads/2015/08/Mueller.pdf (July, 2015). Online; Accessed: 2017-04-10.

[13] IBM Corporation. Big Data & Analytics in the Manufacturing Industry: The Vaasan Group. `https://www.slideshare.net/IBMBDA/ibm-bda-vassangroupslidesharefinal` (2014). Online; Accessed: 2017-04-10.

[14] SAP. Internet of Things. `http://go.sap.com/solution/internet-of-things.html` Online; Accessed: 2016-06-22.

[15] Microsoft Corporation. Azure IoT Suite. `https://www.microsoft.com/en-us/cloud-platform/internet-of-things-azure-iot-suite` Online; Accessed: 2016-06-22.

[16] General Electric. GE Launches Brilliant Manufacturing Suite to Help Manufacturers Increase Production Efficiency, Execution and Optimization through Advanced Analytics. `https://www.ge.com/digital/press-releases/ge-launches-brilliant-manufacturing-suite` (Sept., 2015). Online; Accessed: 2016-06-23.

[17] SAS Institute. Manufacturing. `http://www.sas.com/en_us/industry/manufacturing.html` Online; Accessed: 2016-06-23.

[18] R. van der Meulen and J. Rivera. A Quarter Billion Connected Vehicles Will Enable New In-Vehicle Services and Automated Driving Capabilities. `http://www.gartner.com/newsroom/id/2970017` (Jan., 2015). Online; Accessed: 2016-06-14.

[19] R. Viereckl, D. Ahlemann, A. Koster, and S. Jursch. Connected Car Study 2015:
Racing ahead with autonomous cars and digital innovation. `http://www.strategyand.pwc.com/reports/connected-car-2015-study` (Sept., 2015). Online; Accessed: 2016-06-14.

[20] IBM Corporation. Ford, IBM Use Data Analytics to Find More Efficient Ways to Move. `http://www-03.ibm.com/press/us/en/pressrelease/48774.wss` (Jan., 2016). Online; Accessed: 2016-06-21.

[21] M. Murphy. Ford Brakes the Mould with Car Maintenance Prediction Algorithm. `https://tinyurl.com/m6ky3du` (Jan., 2015). Online; Accessed: 2016-06-21.

[22] Daimler AG. Intelligent Driving. `https://www.daimler.com/innovation/efficiency/intelligent-driving.html` Online; Accessed: 2016-06-18.

[23] IBM Corporation. Leading German car manufacturer boosts customer satisfaction using IBM Big Data & Analytics. `https://www-03.ibm.com/press/us/en/pressrelease/43392.wss` (Mar., 2014). Online; Accessed: 2016-06-18.

[24] Computer Sciences Corporation. Volkswagen: On the Road to Big Data with Predictive Marketing in Aftermarket. `https://snapshot.csc.com/auto/insights/101101-volkswagen_on_the_road_to_big_data_with_predictive_marketing` Online; Accessed: 2016-06-16.

[25] P. Gittins. Tesla, big data and industrial disruption. `https://www.capgemini.com/blog/insights-data-blog/2015/09/tesla-big-data-and-industrial-disruption` (Sept., 2015). Online; Accessed: 2016-06-16.

[26] W. Grayson. Caterpillar's predictive diagnostics will enable more "repairs before failure" in future telematics updates. `http://www.equipmentworld.`

`com/caterpillar-predictive-diagnostics-telematics/` (Mar., 2015). Online; Accessed: 2016-06-20.

[27] M. Jeske, M. Grüner, and F. Weiß. BIG DATA IN LOGISTICS: A DHL perspective on how to move beyond the hype. `http://www.dhl.com/content/` `dam/downloads/g0/about_us/innovation/CSI_Studie_BIG_DATA.pdf` (Dec., 2013). Online; Accessed: 2016-06-19.

[28] N. Lomas. Amazon Patents "Anticipatory" Shipping To Start Sending Stuff Before You've Bought It. `https://techcrunch.com/2014/01/18/` `amazon-pre-ships/` (Jan., 2014). Online; Accessed: 2016-06-19.

[29] N. Gilbert. Rules tighten on use of antibiotics on farms. `http://www.nature.` `com/news/rules-tighten-on-use-of-antibiotics-on-farms-1.9761` (Jan., 2012).

[30] D. A. Wangler, Aktivitätsmessung zur brunsterkennung – möglichkeiten und nutzen, *Landeskontrollverband für Leistungs- und Qualitütsprüfung Sachsen-Anhalt e.V.* (Nov., 2009).

[31] L. Beringhoff, Kau-sensoren melden die brunst, *top agrar* (2014).

[32] Berkemeier, Ostermann-Palz, and Stöcker, Kuh-navis fr den stall, *Elite Magazin* (2015).

[33] Gartner, Inc. Gartner special report "digital business technologies". `http://` `www.gartner.com/newsroom/id/2839717` (Sept., 2016). Online; Accessed: 2016-06-25.

[34] N. Jurran. Heizkrperthermostat: Eve thermo, *Magazin für Computertechnik c't.* **11**, 48 (May, 2016).

[35] N. Jurran. Bluetooth smart home, *Magazin für Computertechnik c't.* **15**, 59 (June, 2015).

[36] N. Jurran. Homekits anknipser, *Magazin für Computertechnik c't.* **14**, 56 (June, 2016).

[37] S. Hansen. Harke, schlauch, handy, *Magazin für Computertechnik c't.* **13**, 62 (June, 2016).

[38] E. Betters. Apple homekit and home app: What are they and how do they work? `https://tinyurl.com/kcx7c84` (June, 2016). Online; Accessed: 2016-06-26.

[39] Datameer, Inc. Vivint Drives Smart Home Automation With Datameer. `https://www.datameer.com/wp-content/uploads/2015/09/vivint_` `testimonial.pdf` Online; Accessed: 2017-04-20.

[40] Nest Labs. `https://nest.com/` Online; Accessed: 2017-04-24.

[41] S. Hansen. Das gateway – mediolas smart-home-hub, *Magazin fr Computertechnik c't.* **9**, 67 (Apr., 2016).

Index

Printed in the United States
by Bookmasters

Printed in the United States
By Bookmasters